PASTECRAFT

by Mary Lou Cook

with a section on

Calligraphy

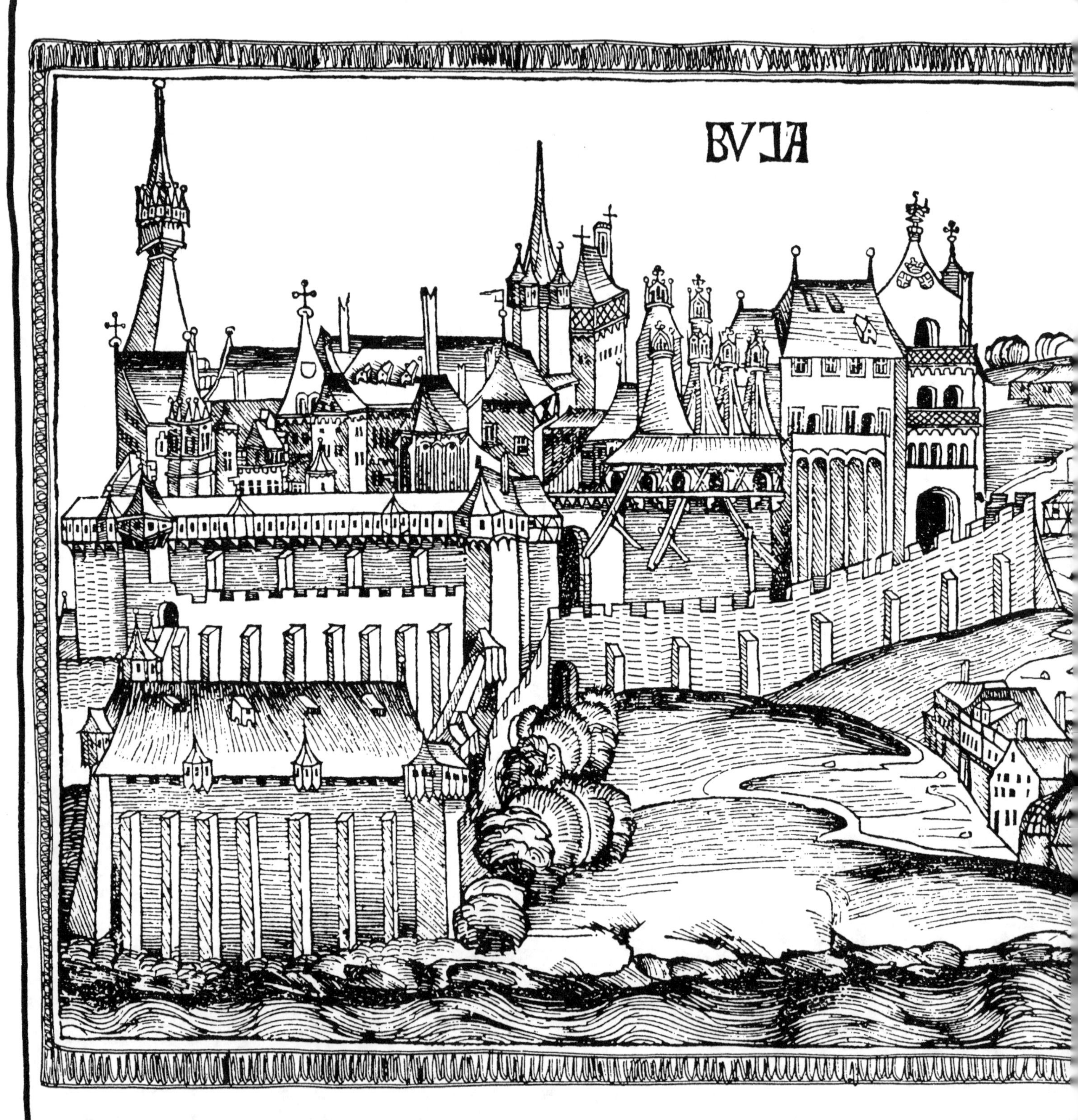
BVDA

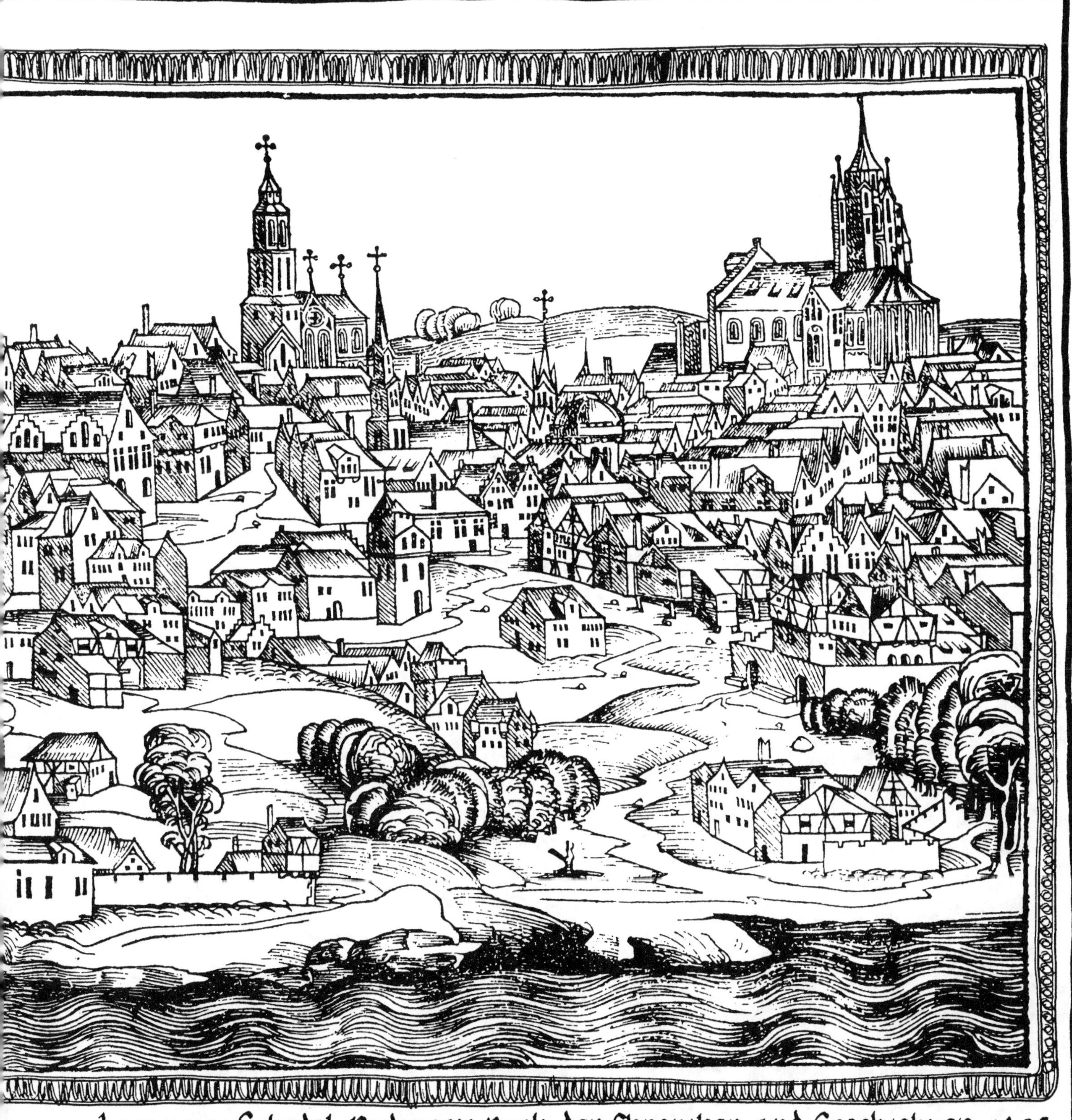

Hartmann Schedel · Budapest · Buch der Chroniken und Geschichten · 1493 ·

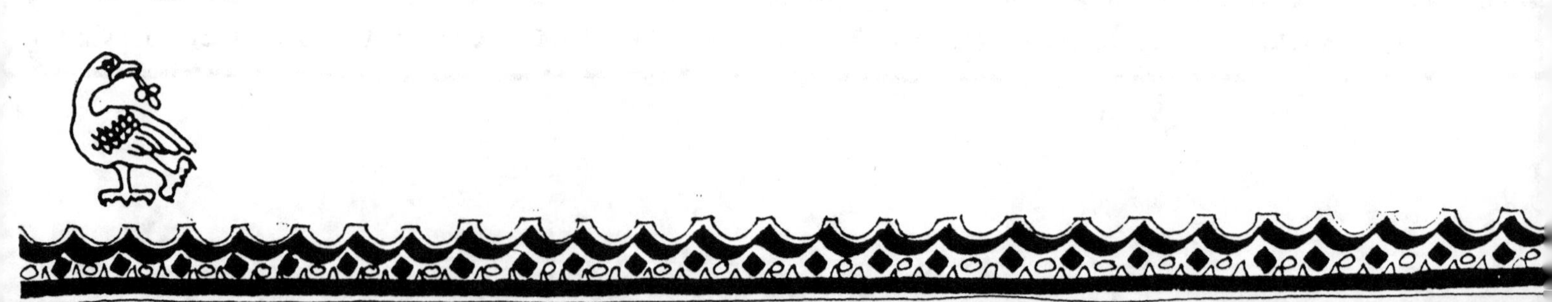

PASTECRAFT

by MARY LOU COOK

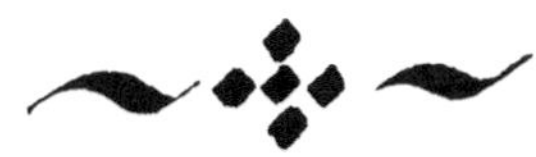

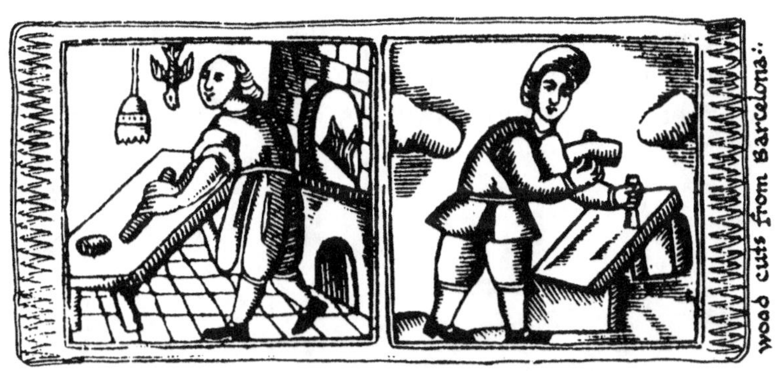

with a section on

Calligraphy

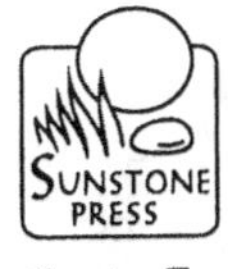

Santa Fe

Book design by Douglas Houston
Back cover photograph by Len Bouché
Mary Lou Cook sketch by Cyrus Leroy Baldridge
Santo research, text and drawing by Andrea Bacigalupa

Sunstone books may be purchased for educational, business, or sales promotional use. For information please write: Special Markets Department, Sunstone Press, P.O. Box 2321, Santa Fe, New Mexico 87504-2321.

Library of Congress Cataloging-in-Publication Data:

Cook, Mary Lou.
Pastecraft: with a section on calligraphy / by Mary Lou Cook
p. cm.
ISBN: 0-86534-342-X
1. Textile crafts. 2. Paste. 3. Shellac. 4. House furnishings.
5. Calligraphy. I. Title.

TT699 .C66 2001
747—dc21 2001049134

Published in

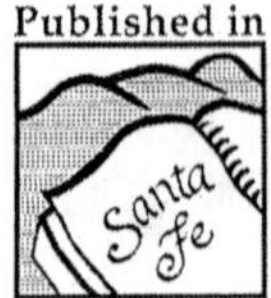

SUNSTONE PRESS
Post Office Box 2321
Santa Fe, NM 87504-2321 / USA
(505) 988-4418 / *orders only* (800) 243-5644
FAX (505) 988-1025
www.sunstonepress.com

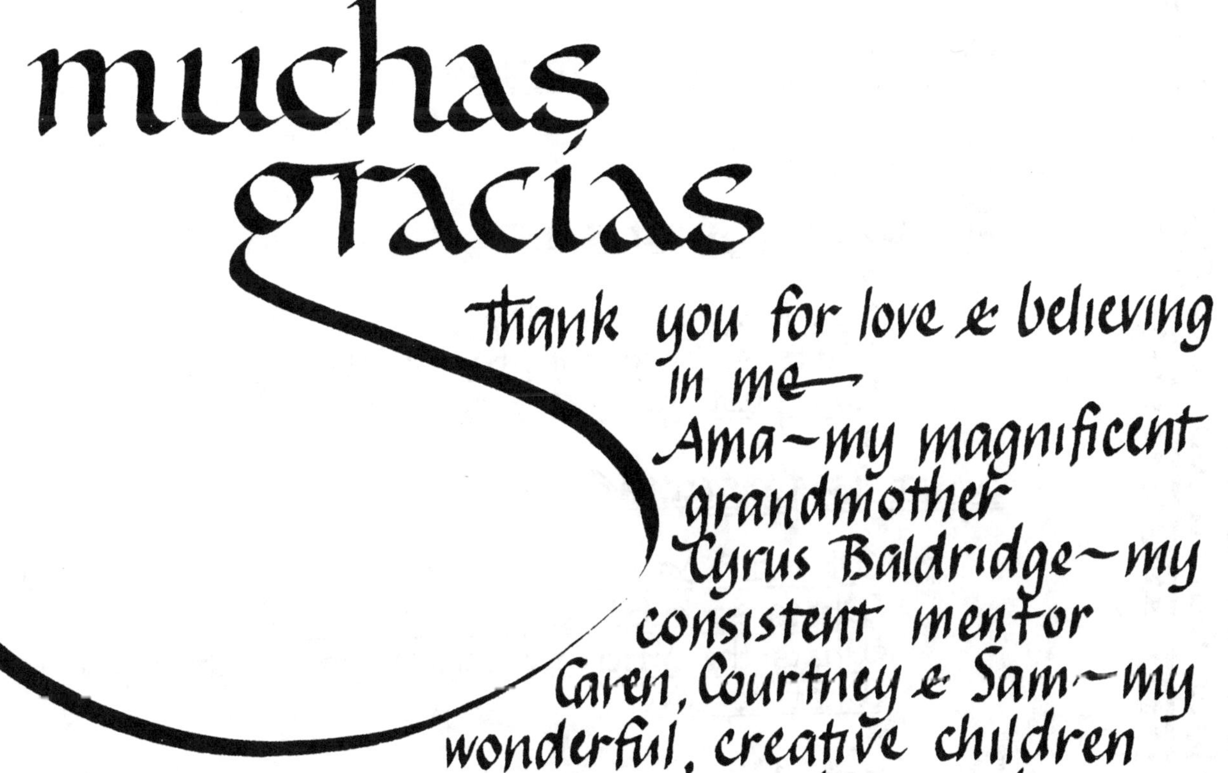

muchas gracias

thank you for love & believing
in me—
Ama—my magnificent
grandmother
Cyrus Baldridge—my
consistent mentor
Caren, Courtney & Sam—my
wonderful, creative children
and Pasters everywhere—who
helped write this book

TABLE OF CONTENTS

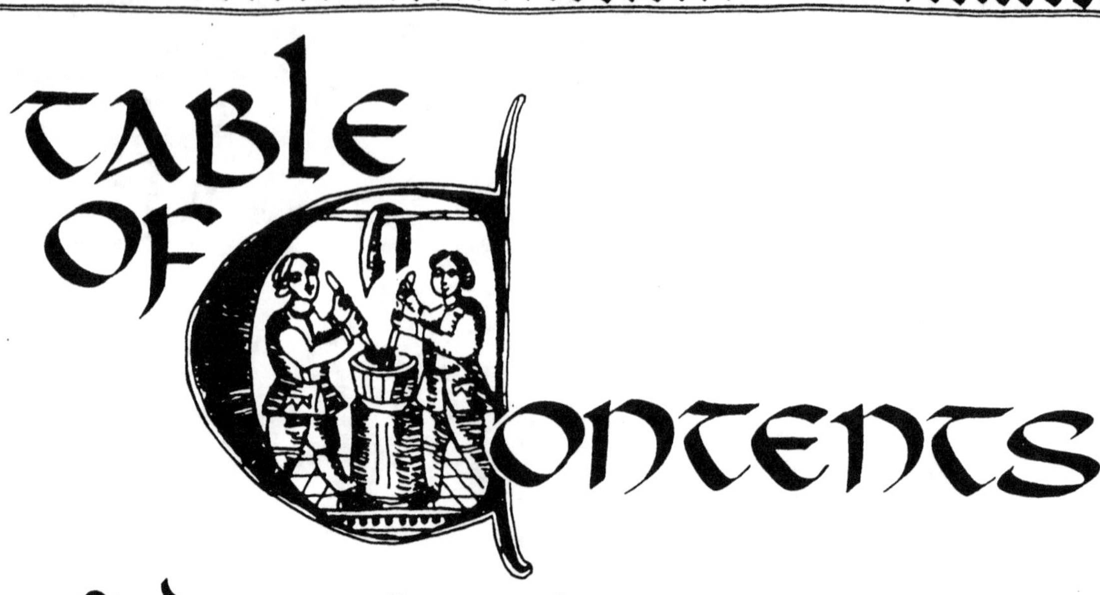

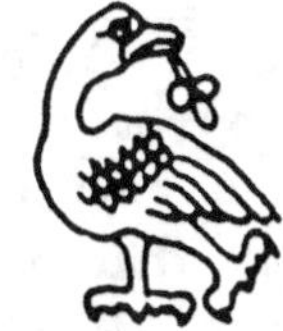

Teach only love, for that is what you are ❖ This instant is the only time there is ❖

A Patron Saint for Craftsmen

Though little known or discussed in America today, St. Dunstan is universally recognized as the patron of Craftsmen. A celebrated, respected & powerful figure in 10th century England, he was appointed abbot of the monastery at Glastonbury, which he turned into the greatest learning center of Europe; & later, under King Edgar, became Bishop of Canterbury, serving as chief adviser to the king in matters of church & state & earning the designation of first Prime Minister of England.

Despite these stately honors, contemporaries wrote most often of Dunstan's humility & of his skill with various crafts in the service of the church. He designed & made bells & sacred vessels, was a scribe who illuminated his own manuscripts, painted, wrote music, played the harp, was an excellent goldsmith & metal worker. He shared with craftsmen of all time the belief that good design is primary & that the work of one's hands — should be functional, serve a purpose. Never a dilettante, arts & crafts were for him no esoteric diversion but the practical techniques through which to supply & surround ourselves with products essential to daily life. Craftsmanship, then as now, was good & honest labour to make these essentials as true & beautiful as our talents allow.

Dunstan's humility is renowned. A manuscript illustration attributed to him features a drawing of Christ on which a self-portrait of the saint, small & inconspicuous, kneels prostrated before the source of all gifts & talents. But he was also resolute against the intrigues, jealousies & libels of the king's court feuds & ambitions among which he moved; & a man to be reckoned with. A popular legend tells us that once while Dunstan was engaged in metal work, the Devil persisted in tempting him, causing Dunstan to use his blacksmith's pincers to still the demon!"

The merciful & gracious Lord hath made a remembrance of his marvellous works." These deathbed words of Dunstan's can be interpreted as the craftsman's heritage — the gift to remember, honor & celebrate, through the work of our hands, the glory of man in God's universe.

In Santa Fé, the royal city dedicated to the holy faith of St. Francis, Dunstan's ideals & standards of craftsmanship live on. Spanish woodcarvers, Indian workers with wool or silver & turquoise, gringo potters & metal workers — the kaleidoscope collage of dedicated artists & craftsmen — labor diligently to fashion products which serve us & are beautiful to the senses. Here in this community where the folk art of the santero — those carvings & paintings executed by untrained artisans for their churches — has commanded worldwide admiration, Dunstan is a welcome member to the long roster of New Mexican patron santos. Feast Day: May 19

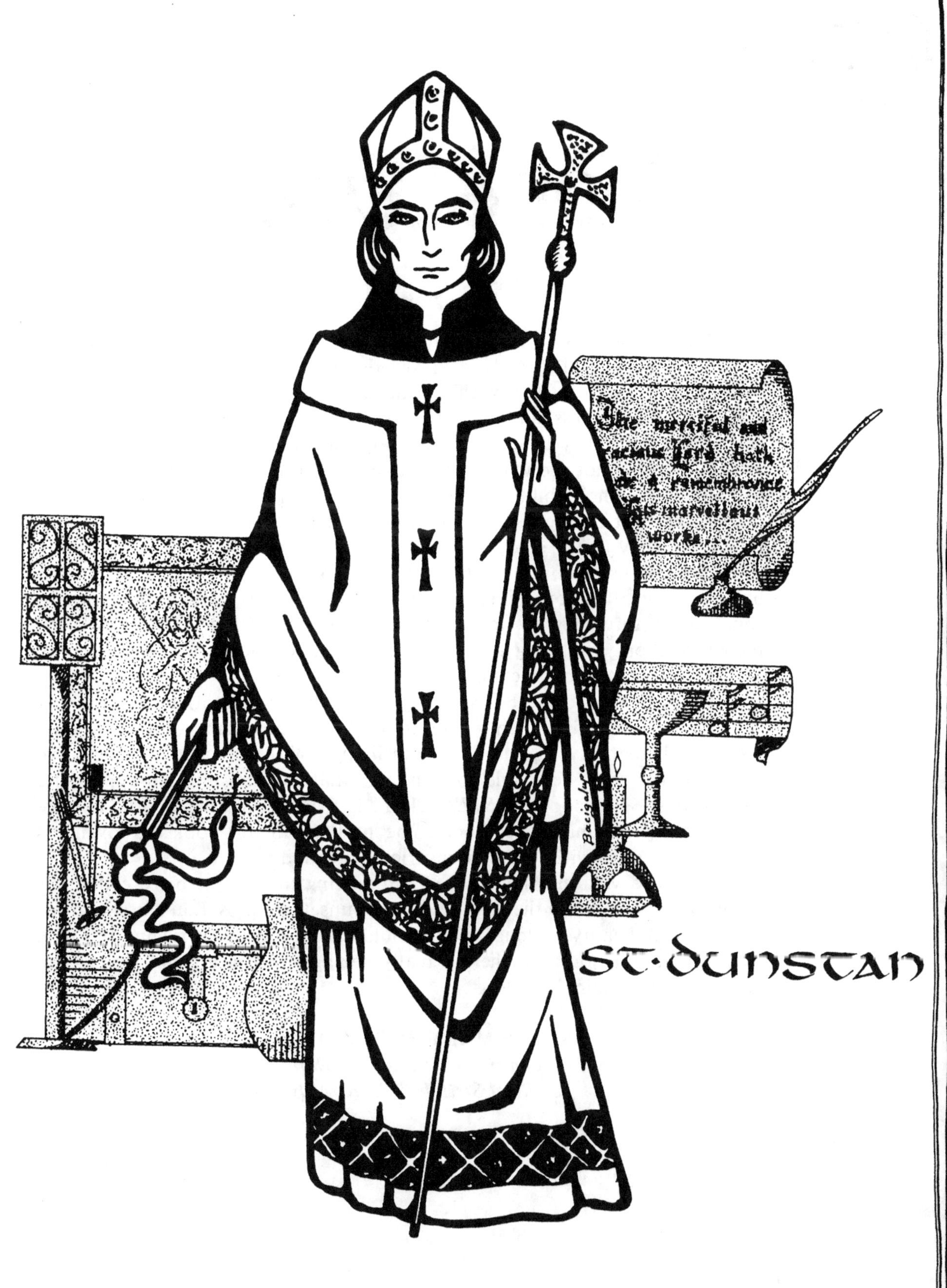
The merciful and
racious Lord hath
de a remembrance
his marvellous
works...
Bacigalupa
ST·DUNSTAN

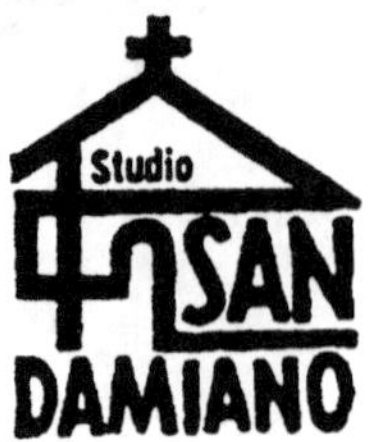

Foreword

"The artist is not a special kind of man, but every man is a special kind of artist" (Eric Gill). Artistic knowledge is gained through the senses by being keenly aware of the world about us. This all-important sensitivity is made up of awareness, an ability to absorb, an eagerness to explore. Imagination and sensitivity lie dormant in many individuals like seed lying in sand or rock that cannot grow unless it is exposed to light, air and water. When individuals use their ability to create, the eyes not only look, but they *see*; the ears are not only conscious of sound, but they *hear*; the hands not only touch, but they *feel*.

Most of us seldom experience tremendous, dramatic encounters with beauty. But all of our lives, humdrum as they may sometimes seem, are touched continuously by rare and charming bits of life. The trick is to recognize them and bring them into our consciousness. We must become seekers of elegance in the commonplace.

It has been a joy to be associated with Mary Lou, both in the teaching field and as a very dear friend. During our long acquaintance, I have become aware of her ability to find beauty in living. With her poetic and creative mind she has truly been able to translate what she sees into happy, artistic expressions. Her book, *PASTECRAFT*, is evidence of her ability to take simple materials and make them come to life. In this book lies loveliness at your fingertips with joyful discoveries all around.

Like the villager who reached out to ring the steeple bells, calling his countrymen to admire the beauties of the sunset, so Mary Lou has contained her ideas of beauty as long as she could, and now she is ringing the bell, asking that you join with her in really seeing and hearing and feeling and working with inspired hands.

SISTER MARY THOMASITA O.S.F.
Chairman, Studio San Damiano
Cardinal Stritch College, Milwaukee

MLC

INTRODUCTION

When the idea of this book began to take form, one of my students, an enthusiastic Paster, suggested that I call it "A Creative Craft for the Non-Creative." It was a good idea and might even have sold books, but it just isn't true. There is no such thing as a non-creative person! EVERYONE HAS CREATIVE ABILITY. Most of us just don't take the time to discover it.

How often have we heard someone say, "I'm all thumbs," or "I can't draw a straight line with a ruler," or "I have no talent," or "I don't have any ideas?" There is just one answer to statements like that: take a risk, give yourself a chance. You'll be surprised by what ten thumbs can accomplish and with the first few pieces you'll realize the satisfaction of making something with your hands.

Follow me through PASTECRAFT and let's discover together that creative person inside you.

Mary Lou Cook

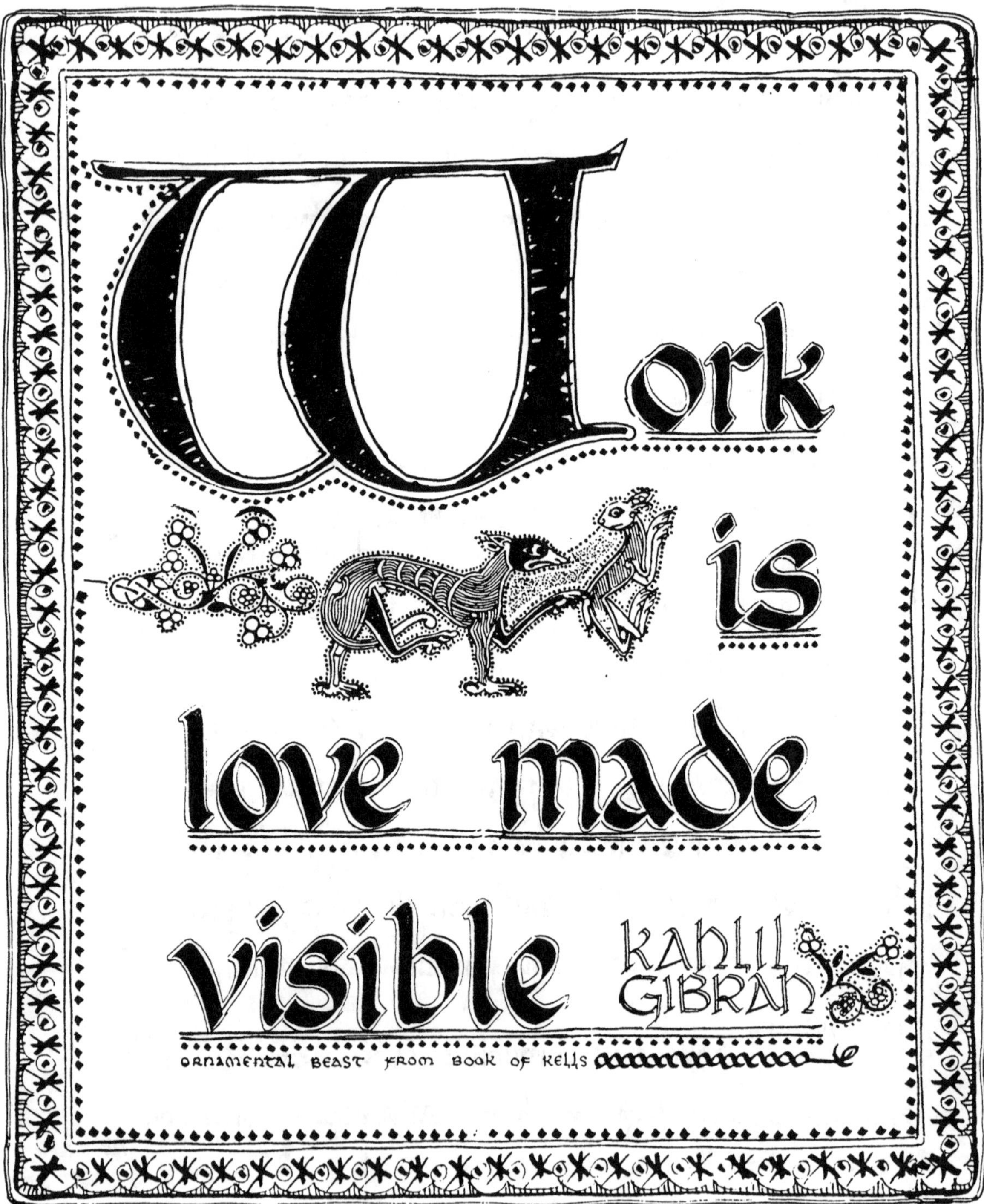
Work
is
love made
visible
KAHLIL
GIBRAN
ORNAMENTAL BEAST FROM BOOK OF KELLS

The Why of Crafts

It is my firm belief, a guiding principle of my life, that everyone has creativity within. Since it is in man's nature to create, it follows that everyone should have a creative outlet. If human beings do not have a creative experience every day or so they are not fulfilling their humanness. They become dry and empty and eventually there is a withering. We should expose ourselves to every creative possibility and experience that comes our way. Through persistent searching, sooner or later the one thing (or the dozen things) meant for you will emerge.

The purpose of a creative outlet is to *re-create* the self through happy and satisfying experiences. By diving into a project and losing yourself for a time, however brief, you can then go on more relaxed. Through your creative experiences you can learn to live with a new joy, bringing from the work table a revitalized sense of your own worth.

There's great satisfaction to be gained from work. And that is why we must never confuse creativity with hobbies. A *hobby*, according to my dictionary, is something a person likes to do in his spare time. Creativity should never be something you do in your spare time. It must be a part of your life, indulged in not when you have the time but when you take the time.

Of all the forms of creativity, crafts are one of the major outlets easily available to everyone. Crafts generally require simple procedures for the production of useful and decorative objects. Most crafts start with a basic set of rules. The same skills are required for building a plain wooden box as for a delicately constructed Chippendale desk. The difference lies in the individual's inherent talent, ability and experience. Not everyone can build the desk, but you'll never know what you can do until you've at least tried to make the box.

That is why you must keep experimenting until you find the creative outlet meant for you. Pastecraft may be that outlet. It requires no particular skills yet offers limitless possibilities. You are bound only by your own imagination. For years I have taught and shared pastecraft with all sorts of people. My classes have included college graduates, elementary school pupils, housewives, professional people and mentally retarded children. I have watched hundreds of my students come alive in the realization of their ability to create something beautiful. Those ten thumbs slowly evolve into two thumbs and eight fingers capable of molding an original creation out of bits and pieces.

Another benefit of having a creative outlet is to help fill a void caused by withdrawal from tobacco, drugs or alcohol, strict dieting or a a long convalescence. The secret of mental health is to find interest in something other than oneself and to undertake things with zest and enthusiasm.

ENCOURAGING CREATIVITY

First of all, to encourage creativity, you will need a *Worktable.* Every home should have one. It can be a card table or a picnic table or any other kind just so it is designated "worktable." But it should never be the kitchen or dining table which has to be cleared for meals. Your work area should always be free and ready for you with several shelves for supplies, good light and your favorite music.

With the worktable goes creativity. It produces a mood and you will find that just sitting down to it will help you get started. Some of the most meaningful things in my life have happened there.

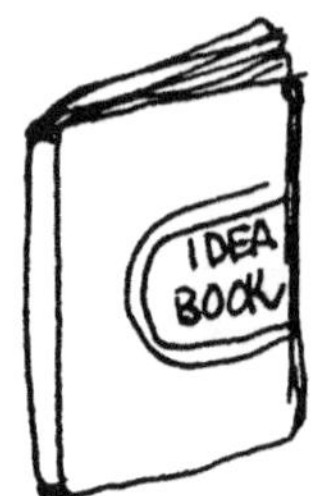

The second thing you need is an *Idea Book.* An old-fashioned scrapbook, a bound volume of blank pages, a notebook – whatever you like will suffice. Into it you paste ideas, pictures, thoughts, poems, proverbs – whatever speaks to you. From this book will come your ideas for projects.

Maggy Ryan
"THE OWL"
ALBRECHT DÜRER
MCMLXXIV

The third thing required for the encouragement of creativity is your *Signature.* Sign everything you make! Your name on an object says, "I made this and I'm proud of it." You worked hard and the results are a pleasing or useful item. Modesty is unbecoming because if a thing is not worth signing it is not worth keeping. You'll find in time that even the thought of signing your work will make you try a little harder.

The fourth ingredient called for is *Experimentation.* Be inventive, try new things – difficult things, easy things. Be prepared to make mistakes but don't worry about those things you finally have to throw away. You'll learn more from mistakes than from successes. It is frequently difficult to remember how you did a thing correctly, but you'll never forget how you botched a job. Through experimentation you will open new doors, find new paths and today's dabbling may become tomorrow's creative outlet.

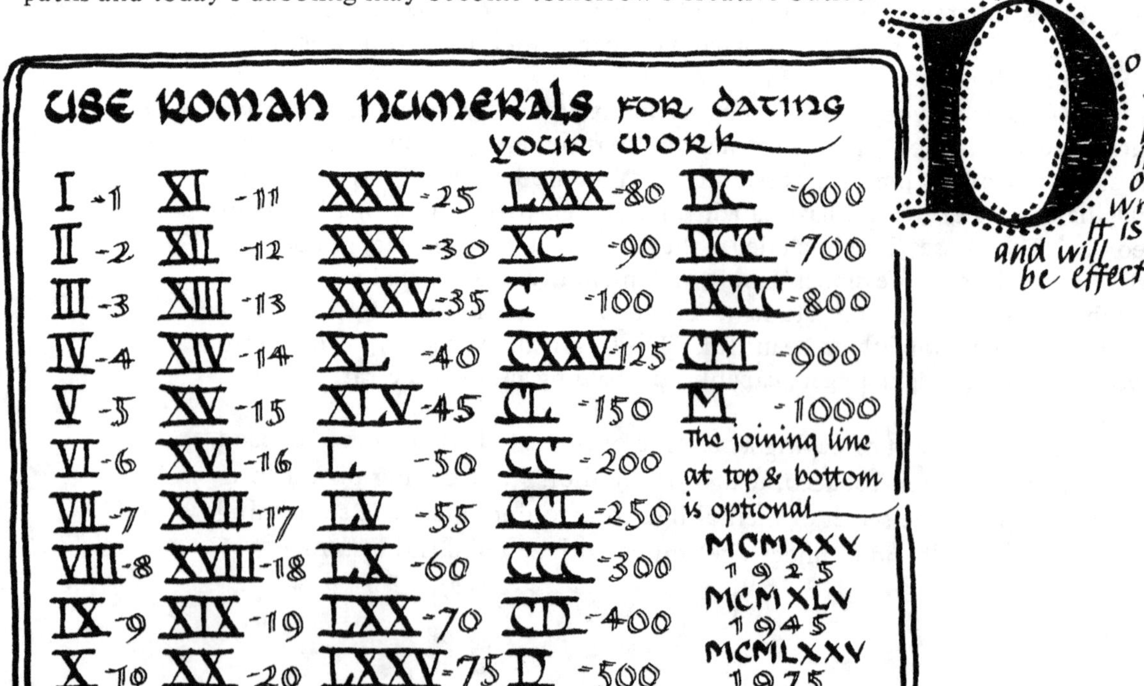

Do any signatures or lettering in your own handwriting. It is you and will be effective.

HOW PASTECRAFT CAME TO BE AND HOW IT GREW

Working with my hands has been a way of life as long as I can remember. I have a rich heritage in that my two grandmothers and my mother did handwork. It seemed natural to me to invent, to work things out, to improvise. I read and dreamed, sewed and knitted and involved my family in projects. One such project, which my brother and sister have never forgotten nor forgiven, was making a badminton net, knot by knot by knot by knot by knot by knot by knot. . . .It was never finished.

The idea of Pastecraft was germinated by a bookbinding course in 1935 at the University of Kansas, taught by Professor Rosemary Ketcham, where I learned to make the paste formula which is used to put leather bindings on the hardboard covers of books. The recipe is centuries old, strong and binding and has been used since early days by European bookbinders.

In the early days of my marriage there was little money for wedding, birthday and Christmas gifts, so once again I began to improvise. After determining that the paste wouldn't spot fabric, I covered pieces of plywood with gingham and paste, shellacked them and attached brass window pulls for handles. These trays were the first product of pastecraft and the beginning of a new creative activity.

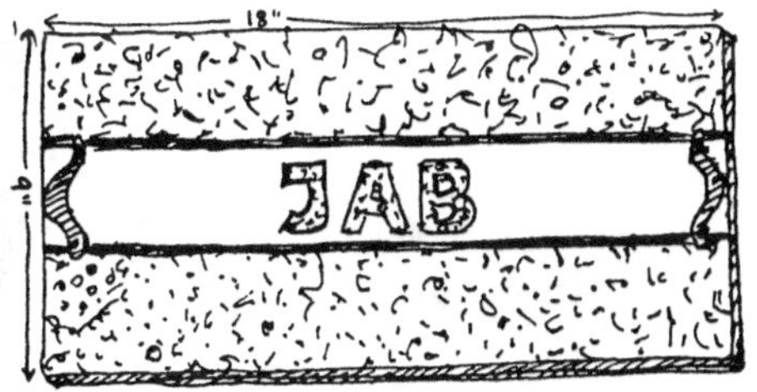

Several years, many business moves and three children later, there was still no money for gifts. But by then, the making of gifts and home decorations had become a way of life. I realized that the only real gift is a part of oneself and enormous satisfaction can be derived from creating warm, personal and unique home surroundings.

At some point it occurred to me that here was a new technique. Later, I put a name to it, and still later started giving classes. For a number of years now I've given Pastecraft workshops all over the country, receiving enthusiastic response.

See Quotes from Pasters

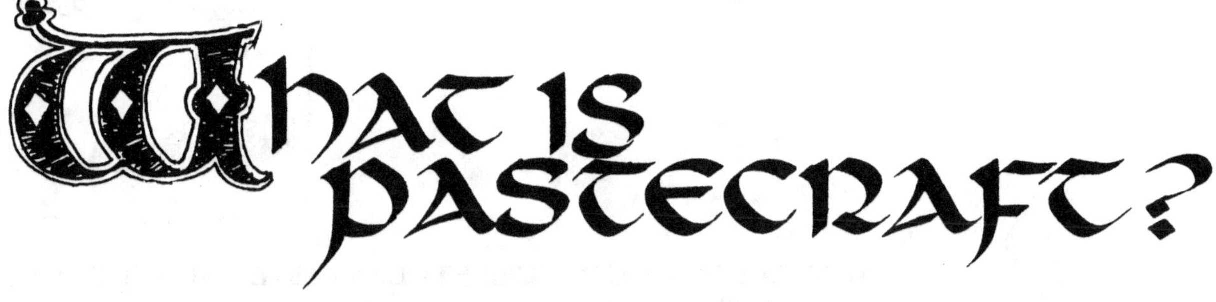

Pastecraft is a folk art of today, for the "veriest beginner." It is the simple art of working with fabric, paste and shellac to cover surfaces and solid objects. It is a wonderful way to inject new life into almost anything, offering practical and ingenious solutions to home decorating problems and inexpensive means of making beautiful heirlooms and gifts. It is a "no-fail" craft for the person who believes he can't work with his hands, giving him a new and needed self-confidence.

It helps develop an *attitude* toward creative living and thinking by imparting a spirit of fun, humor and enjoyment. Pastecraft is a pleasant and delightful skill that may be used for the rest of one's life.

Pastecraft emphasizes practicality and thriftiness in that it's not necessary to buy new furniture or decorative items to work with. The main thing is to look for good lines and design in an object – which means chances of discovering great "finds" at garage sales, secondhand stores and in giveaways from unimaginative relatives and friends.

Pastecraft is the combined use of head, heart & hands

WHO CAN DO PASTECRAFT?

Its adaptability is demonstrated by the fact that while Pastecraft is for the "veriest beginner," it is also for the experienced craftsman. This technique can be used along with other skills with a high degree of expertise and excellence to produce quality creative work.

this is a winning ribbon · color it blue

WHAT'S SO GOOD ABOUT THIS PASTE?

1. It's easy to make.
2. It's inexpensive; the flour, sugar and water cost only a few cents a pint.
3. It won't spot cotton fabrics.
4. It has a strong adhesive quality. Bookbinders have long used this formula for pasting leather over cardboard in making book covers. Our grandmothers also cooked it for restless kids to use in craft work.
5. It's easy to apply to fabric with a brush.
6. It acts as a filler in the cloth and produces a hard surface when dry.
7. It's handy for household repairs.
8. It is the agent that allows fabric to be stretched and manipulated.
9. It is similar to wallpaper paste, but cheaper and better.
10. It is great for papier-mâché.
11. It's fun to work with!

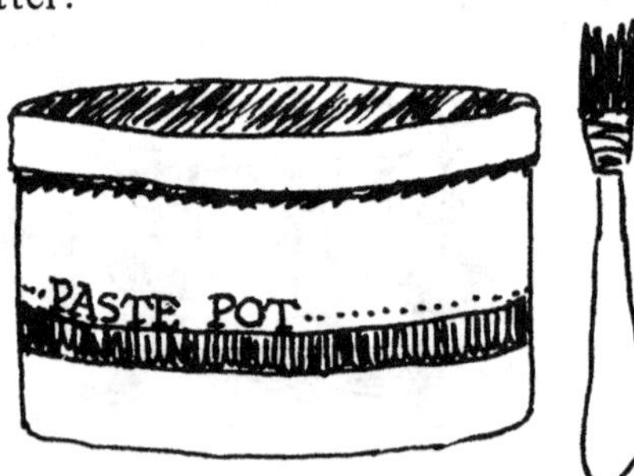

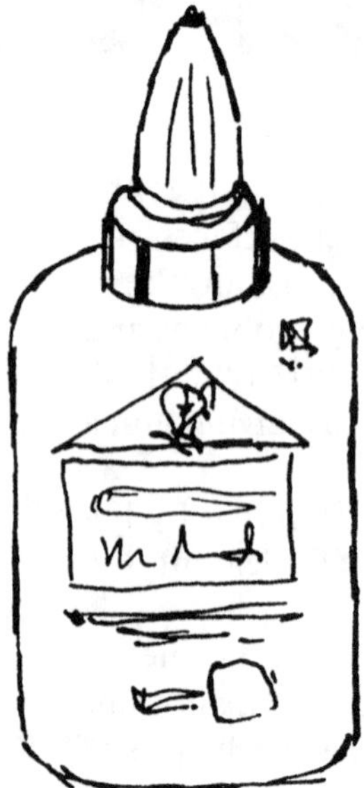

WHAT'S THE DIFFERENCE BETWEEN PASTE AND WHITE GLUE?

A lot!!! It's important to understand the proper use of each, as both are necessary for good craftsmanship, or may I say pastemanship? By white glue I mean Elmer's, Fuller's, Duratite and other polyvinyl resin products. Paste is to be used on fabric as it won't spot and makes possible a smooth, professional job. It is excellent for covering solid, firm surfaces of wood, glass, porcelain, tin, cement, stone, plastic, etc. It should not be used on cardboard as the moisture in the paste will cause warping unless the cardboard is pressed under a heavy weight until dry. (Exceptions: lamp shades, wastebaskets.)

White glue is used for attaching braids, decorations and dimensional objects that protrude from the surface. Liquitex Polymer medium is similar to white glue and may be used instead. It should not be used on fabrics, as it will spot, look shiny and dry too fast for working. When I refer to *paste* and *glue* – remember there is a difference!

WHAT TO COVER?

Use your ingenuity in selecting objects to cover, keeping in mind that they should be sturdy and have good lines. If it has good line and design, or is functional, it is worth covering. Look closely at basic shapes of things that are worn, old, the wrong color or about to be discarded. Likely things may be close at hand. It's up to you to see the possibilities of refurbishing such things as lampshades, picture frames, metal trays, scarred table tops, bridge table tops, wooden chairs, benches, folding screens, wastebaskets, wooden drawers, closet accessories, an "impossible" floor, doors, walls, ceilings, bathrooms, a window that needs an opaque cover other than a curtain, trunks, window frames, wall panels, cabinet fronts, suitcases, dolls – the list is endless!

GARAGE SALE
ALL KINDS OF JUNK • CHEAP

You'll want to save small things that can be used for gifts and decorative accessories such as boxes, jars, bottles, saucers, tin cans, books, bread boxes and cannister sets.

Please note that I don't suggest covering things of value or things in good condition. It would be unwise to cover a fine hardwood floor, a hand-bound book, a good door – and, please, don't cover too many objects in one pattern for a single room.

Pasting Particulars

PREPARING SURFACE, MENDING, ETC.

The object to be covered must be structurally sound and have a smooth surface. Do all repairs first and let dry before pasting. If a book, lampshade, bridge table, etc., needs strengthening, use a strip of muslin or any scrap of fabric with white glue as the mending agent. This will dry quickly. If working on tin or plastic that is too slick for fabric to adhere to, brush on a coat of shellac which produces a grainy, rough surface that can easily be pasted onto. If covering a metal that may rust when moist paste is applied, such as the lining of an old metal trunk, brush shellac on the surface. When covering a painted object that may fade or discolor, brush shellac on the surface.

My carpenter son says
Plywood won't warp, wood will

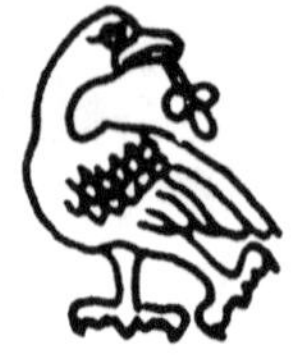

CHOOSING THE RIGHT FABRIC

Look for fabric that reflects your tastes and will look well with your other furnishings. Study the material closely and then view the total effect from a distance. If you have an active family, you would be wise to select a lightweight cotton print that can be shellacked until permanent and waterproof. If you don't have to be practical and prefer an elegant decor, try putting velveteens and rich fabrics on table tops, valances or wall alcoves. As a general rule, these can't be shellacked but will last well.

Start collecting new and used fabrics from garage sales, your friends and remnant tables. Soft, pliable fabrics such as cotton, thin wool, linen, rayon, ginghams and calicos in stripes, checks and prints are the easiest to work with. You may also use textured and rough-woven cloth, such as monk's cloth, heavy rayon or denim. These are hard to handle on a curved surface because of the ravels and heavy edges but are excellent on a flat surface such as a wall or a screen. It is usually best to cut off selvages as they tend to shrink.

Be cautious with silks and synthetics. Silks may spot and synthetics may not absorb the paste. The only way to find out is to try a small piece. Felt has limited use, as it shrinks when pasted, but can be applied as top decoration with white glue. If a fabric is thin or light-colored, the design or color underneath may show through. To test, hold one thickness of dry fabric over object to be covered. It is especially important to check a lampshade for complete effectiveness of fabric. To do this simply drape fabric over the shade and turn on the light.

If you're doing new slipcovers, buy several extra yards so you can use this same fabric on a wastebasket, lampshade, bed headboard or valances – but, please, not too much of the same print in one room. A sentimental idea is to use a child's favorite outgrown print dress for covering a book or picture frame. A beautiful tie, discarded because of a raspberry stain, will make a handsome covering for a bottle. But always make sure you have enough fabric to finish your project.

I have found that small prints and solid colors are the most effective and easiest to work with, but I urge you to trust your own taste. Have confidence in yourself!

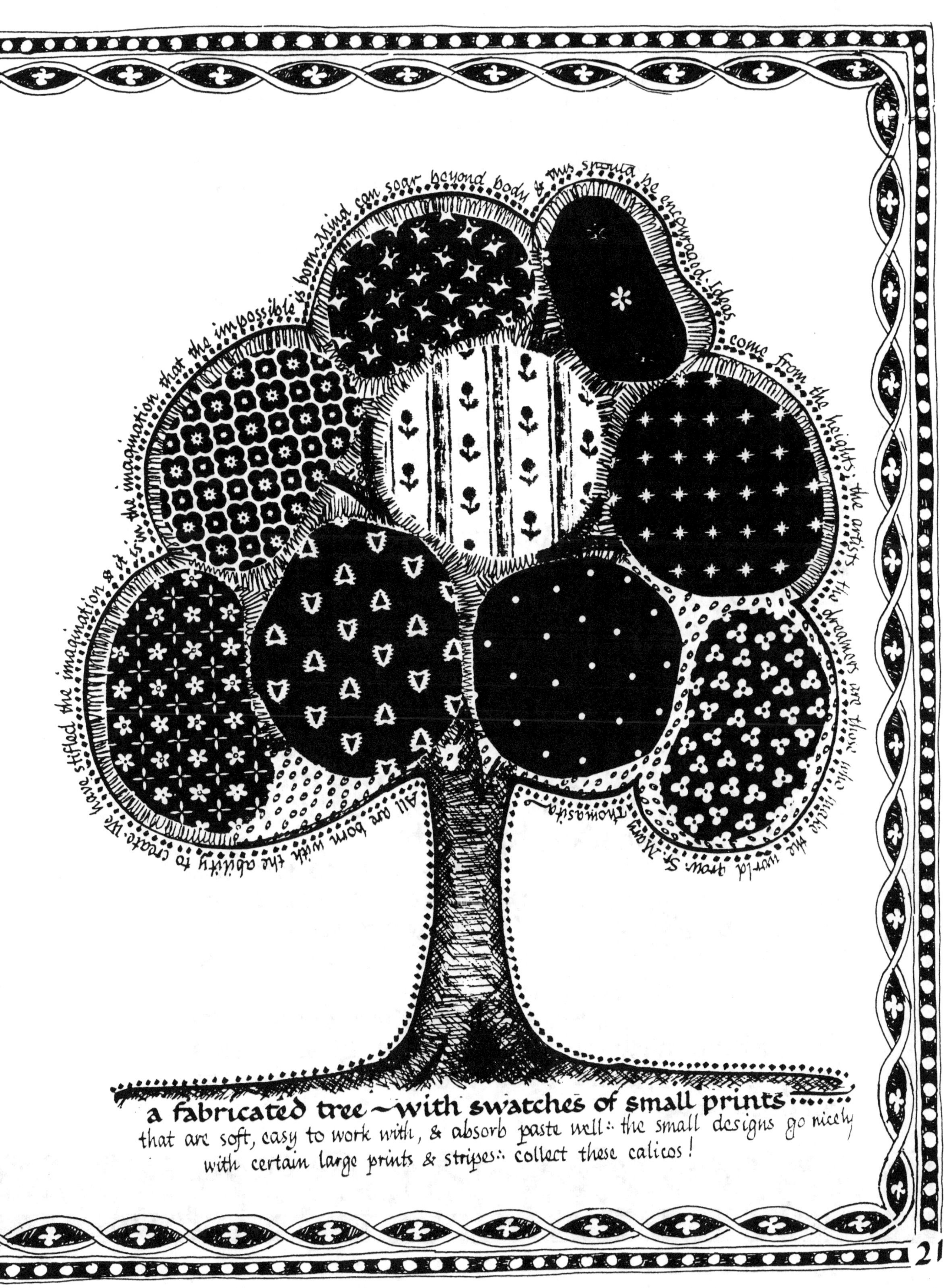

a fabricated tree ~ with swatches of small prints......
that are soft, easy to work with, & absorb paste well: the small designs go nicely with certain large prints & stripes: collect these calicos!

TRIMS

It's good to have a variety of trimmings on hand, such as cotton braid, heavy silk braid, silk seam binding, velvet ribbon, yarn, embroidered tape, fringe, satin ribbon, bias tape, rough jute twine, etc. You can make your own braid by plaiting leather or cotton shoelaces.

PICTURES AND DECORATIONS

Just as the right trim is important in the overall design of your piece, so also is your choice of picture, decoration or design. A picture isn't always necessary, but it may add just the right feel. Start collecting small pictures, prints and designs from magazines, calendars, Christmas cards and postcards of museum reproductions. Be on the lookout for interesting maps, labels from wine bottles, luggage labels, cigar bands, postage stamps, foreign newsprint and special poetry. One clever friend used covers of the *New Yorker* magazine to paper the walls of a small bathroom.

Paper cutout designs

A charming & beautiful folk art called Scherenschnitte (German for scissor-cutting) dates back over 2,200 years. The earliest known work of this kind was done in China & later developed in Germany, Poland, Japan & Mexico. The designs can be as simple or elaborate as the cutter wishes.

Scherenschnitte designs are handsome when used on Pastecraft pieces, such as on book covers, boxes, bottles, lampshades, trays, etc.

Use any paper in any color (gummed paper is available in craft supply shops) Use fingernail scissors for intricate work, otherwise theres no special equipment needed.

Apply the finished design to the fabric with thinned white glue. When dry, spray shellac over the surface for permanence.

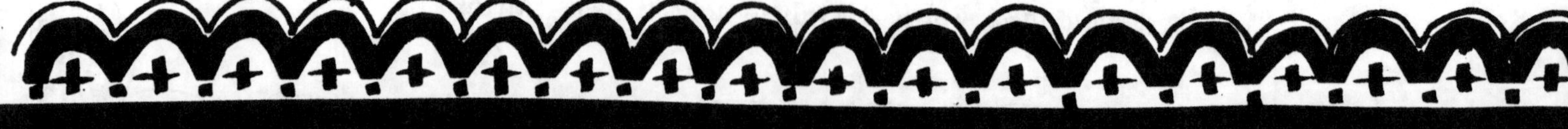

Scherenschnitte

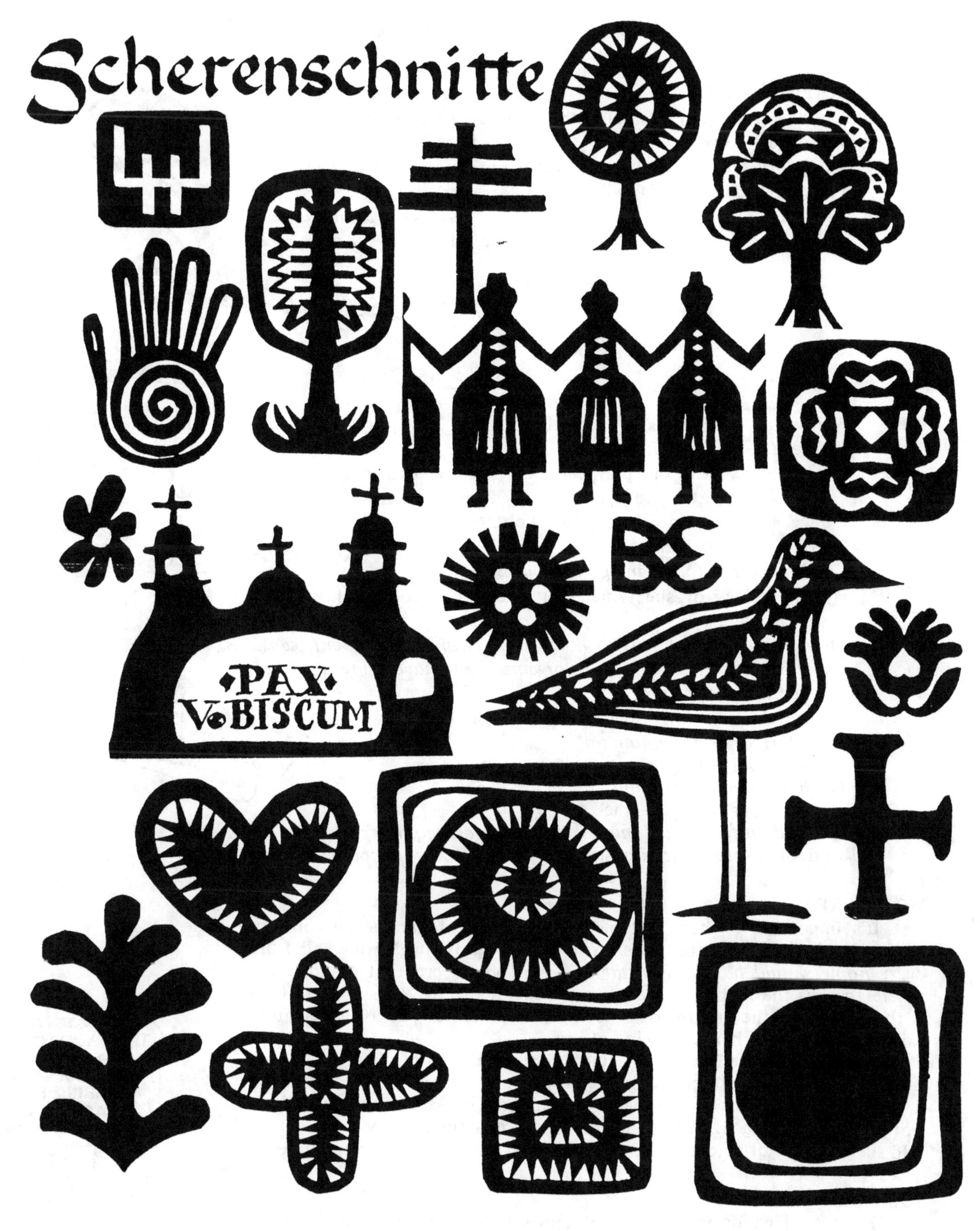

PASTE PARAPHERNALIA

You'll need a minimum of equipment, most of which is available from the dime or hardware store:

2 paint brushes, one inch wide (one for paste, one for shellac).

Paste pot – any glass jar with lid.

Very sharp scissors, any size. This is your one extravagance as wet fabric is hard to cut. Be sure to wipe scissors clean after each use.

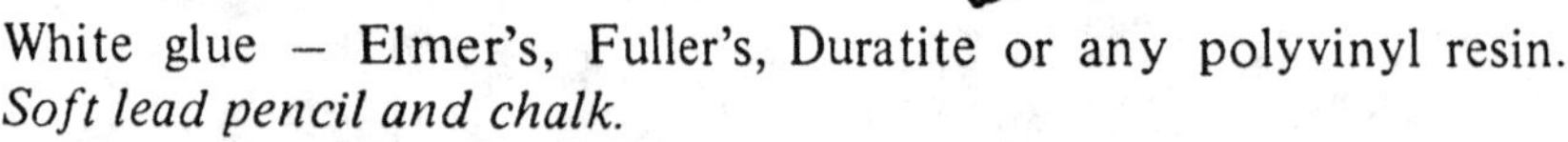

White glue – Elmer's, Fuller's, Duratite or any polyvinyl resin.

Soft lead pencil and chalk.

Clear shellac, bulk or spray can. Bar varnish is also good, as is any agent that is transparent and covers and protects the surface. An alternate is Liquitex Polymer medium or clear nail polish (for small areas).

Alcohol solvent for cleaning shellac brush.

Pressing plates of sheet metal or several flat cookie sheets and several bricks.

Strong corrugated boxes to hold fabric, trims, equipment, cans, bottles, etc. It's good to be organized and have things together when the pasting urge hits you.

Old towels for wiping fingers and for cleaning scissors.

Waxed paper or aluminum foil.

Stacks of old newspapers to protect work surfaces.

Pinch wooden clothes pins.

Foam rubber, 1/4 inch thick.

Serrated knife or small saber saw for projects requiring them.

And, of course, a jar of paste. The recipe appears on page

WORK AREA

It's important to have a table where a project can be left out and worked on in between other jobs. You already know my strong belief that *every home should have a worktable*, a spot where creativity holds forth, where there is the feeling and encouragement of inventiveness, where there is the respect for the "taking risks, trying something new, ideas, imagination, failing, trying it another way" kind of thing.

If no other place is available, find a corner, set up your bridge table and declare this area henceforth to be used by anyone for anything. You'll need a chair, light, wastebasket. Hopefully, if this area is used, it will expand. So you may soon hang a piece of pegboard above it for display purposes and add shelves made of stacked bricks and wooden planks to hold supply boxes.

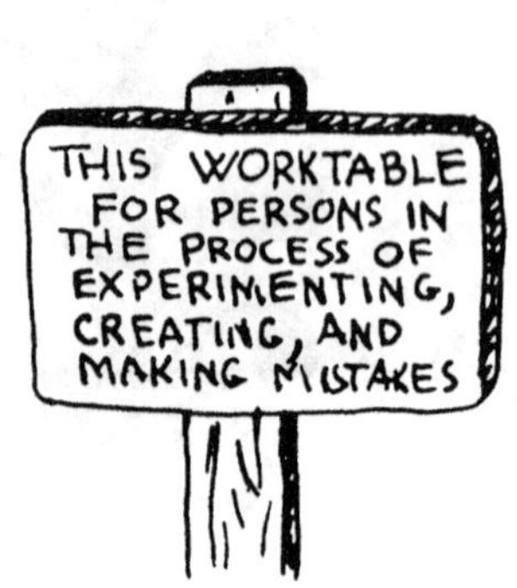

IDEA BOOK

Keep an idea book. In it put things that appeal to you, that give you ideas from which to create. It is helpful for everyone to have such a book. A blank, bound book is better than a looseleaf notebook.

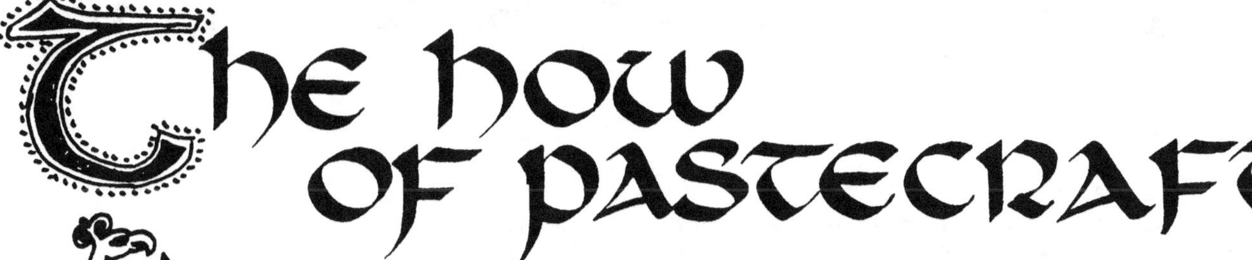

BASIC TECHNIQUES

TO MEASURE FABRIC, allow 1/2 inch extra for small objects and 1 inch extra for large objects (larger than a 10 inch book). Shrinkage of material is no longer any cause to worry, as almost everything is pre-shrunk. But if there is doubt, test for yourself. If it is necessary to mark fabric, do so on the wrong side, using chalk for dark fabric and soft lead pencil for light. Tear fabric when you have a straight line; otherwise use scissors. If using a remnant and your large piece isn't big enough, it is simple to use auxiliary pieces or patches. These won't show if the print or pattern is matched. If a special shape is needed, make a newspaper pattern, cut carefully, then pin onto fabric and cut.

TO APPLY PASTE, spread pad of newspapers on work area; when top paper is messy, throw it away. Lay fabric right side down on paper. Apply paste with brush to wrong side of fabric. Be sure that every bit of fabric is covered with paste and is very wet. It will probably saturate the fabric to the right side, which is what it's supposed to do. Don't be timid about brushing paste onto fabric. Paste with a positive brush.

Now pick up fabric by edges and place on object to be covered or, if easier, lay object on fabric. Starting at the center, smooth and rub with your hands until all bubbles and wrinkles are gone and fabric adheres to every surface area. If a portion of the fabric won't stick, brush paste on front of fabric until it does stick. The torn edge won't show; it clings well to the fabric underneath.

When fitting a curve (and here's the secret of it all), make slashes 1/2 inch apart in the fabric, cutting to where the curve starts. Overlap these pieces one at a time rather firmly and push the fabric flat to the curve. How far to slash? As deep as necessary to eliminate puckers. Trust your eyes. *Always* wipe scissors clean after each use.

DRYING AND PRESSING

It is important that this is done correctly. Be sure that fabric is applied smoothly with no bubbles or wrinkles as it's too late after the fabric is dry. Stand your finished piece on a hard slick surface to dry, such as waxed paper, a cookie tin, the bathroom floor or the metal racks inside the stove. Don't leave on newspapers as they will stick to wet fabric. Don't leave on wooden tabletop as the moisture from the paste will spot the wood.

Paste usually dries within an hour unless several thicknesses of fabric are involved. If you are in a hurry, put in the sun, in a warm oven, or use a hair dryer. When dry, the fabric takes on a hard surface which is caused by the paste acting as a filler in the small woven holes of the cloth.

Some things have to be pressed while drying to keep them from warping. This is particularly true with cardboard. It must be pressed flat with a heavy weight until completely dry. Bricks on cookie sheets do a fine job except for objects like wastebaskets and lampshades.

SHELLACKING

When dry, most things should be shellacked for permanence. Using a brush or spray can, apply several coats of shellac to the surface of fabric. The number of coats depends on the type of finish you want. Be sure to take the same precautions when drying the shellacked piece as were mentioned under drying and pressing. Sticky surfaces should not touch anything. I use a boot-drying rack for bottles, cans, boxes, etc. To shellac over paper printed with ink that may smear, first use two coats of spray shellac to set the ink. Then a third coat can be brushed on without smearing.

Clean your shellac brush with alcohol solvent because turpentine won't work with shellac. You can use clear shellac, which is quite transparent and doesn't change the colors in the fabric, or you can use orange shellac which darkens light colors and gives an antique look. Gold dust may be added to shellac for a different effect. Clear nail polish can be used on small objects instead of shellac.

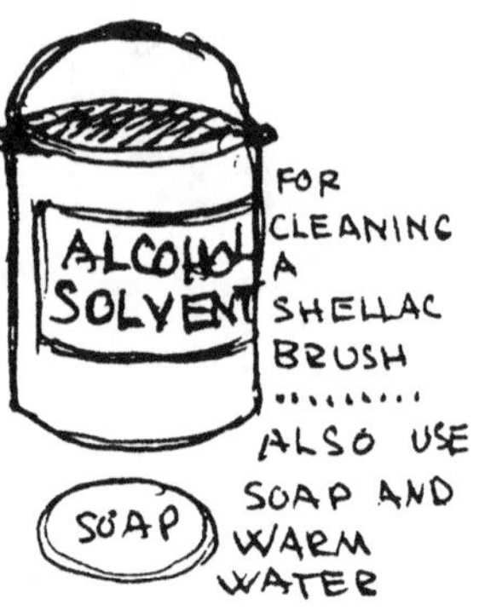

TRIMMING AND DECORATION

When the basic work of covering the object with fabric is done, it's time to decide if any trimming or decoration is needed. Trimming may be applied when fabric is either dry or wet. Consider the contrast or matching of both color and texture. The right trimming used with the right fabric will give your piece a finished look. Here's where your personal taste makes all the difference. The print of a fabric may be strong enough so that you won't need any trimming. Perhaps one row of silk seam binding to cover a raw edge will suffice. Obviously, pictures can't be used in combination with large, strong over-all prints, yet small geometrics or stripes enhance certain pictures. This decision takes thought and experience and comes easier with each piece.

You may want to use a small picture, print or map which can be framed by yarn glued around the edges or sealing wax melted at the borders. You may want to use initials that are cut out of contrasting felt or fabric. You could use several heavy bold braids close together around the edge of an object.

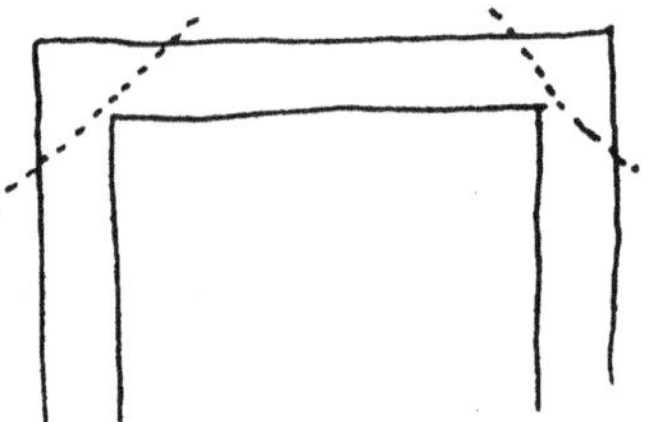

MITERING A CORNER

This process is used in finishing a flat corner or right angle. It is done exactly as the carpenter makes his miter joint with wood in constructing a door or picture frame.

When covering thin cardboard, cut corner of fabric away from cardboard by a straight diagonal line. Leave 1/8 inch extra for overlap so that it covers the cardboard corner.

BUT— I DON'T HAVE ANY IDEAS

How do you get ideas? Once you're into handwork your eye quickly develops and you start looking at things from the viewpoint of the producer. Sister Thomasita phrases it well in her preface. For instance, I've filled my idea book with sketches made at exhibits, museums, libraries, everywhere – from things I've discovered that "speak to me." We can learn so much from the past.

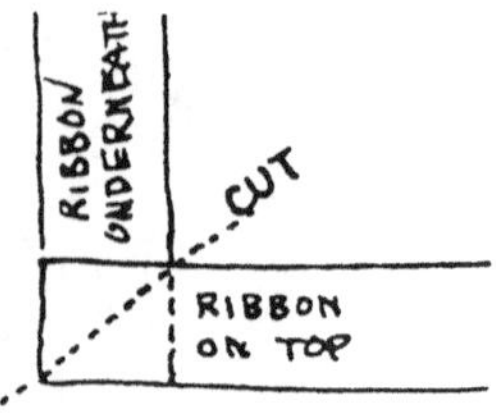

IDEA

To get a neat corner with ribbon, criss-cross the two ribbons and cut diagonally through both, then apply with glue or paste as surface decoration.

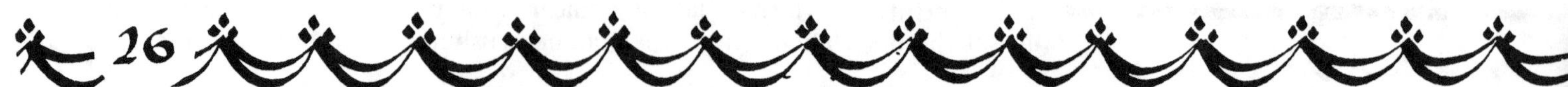

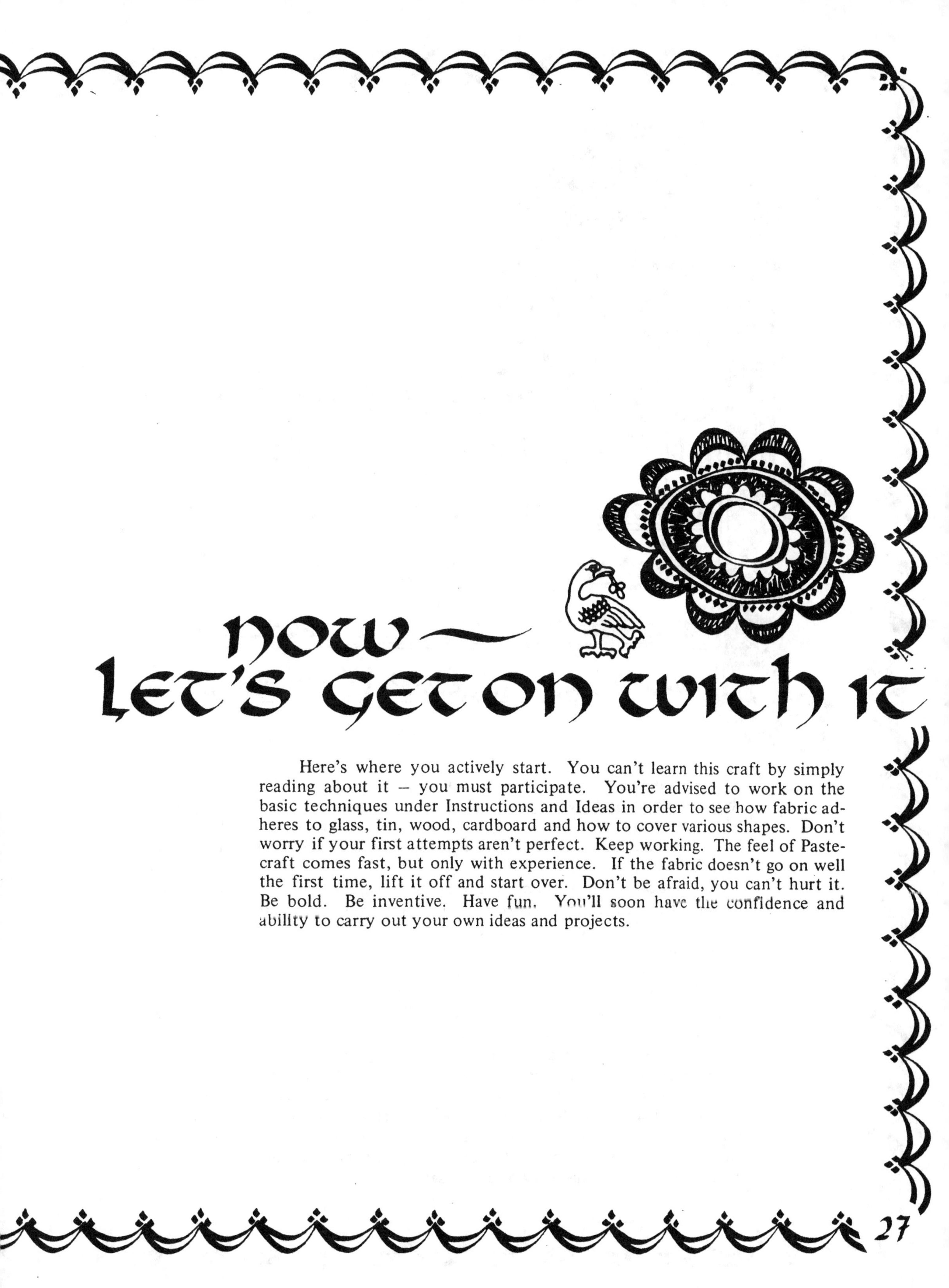

Now — Let's Get On With It

Here's where you actively start. You can't learn this craft by simply reading about it – you must participate. You're advised to work on the basic techniques under Instructions and Ideas in order to see how fabric adheres to glass, tin, wood, cardboard and how to cover various shapes. Don't worry if your first attempts aren't perfect. Keep working. The feel of Pastecraft comes fast, but only with experience. If the fabric doesn't go on well the first time, lift it off and start over. Don't be afraid, you can't hurt it. Be bold. Be inventive. Have fun. You'll soon have the confidence and ability to carry out your own ideas and projects.

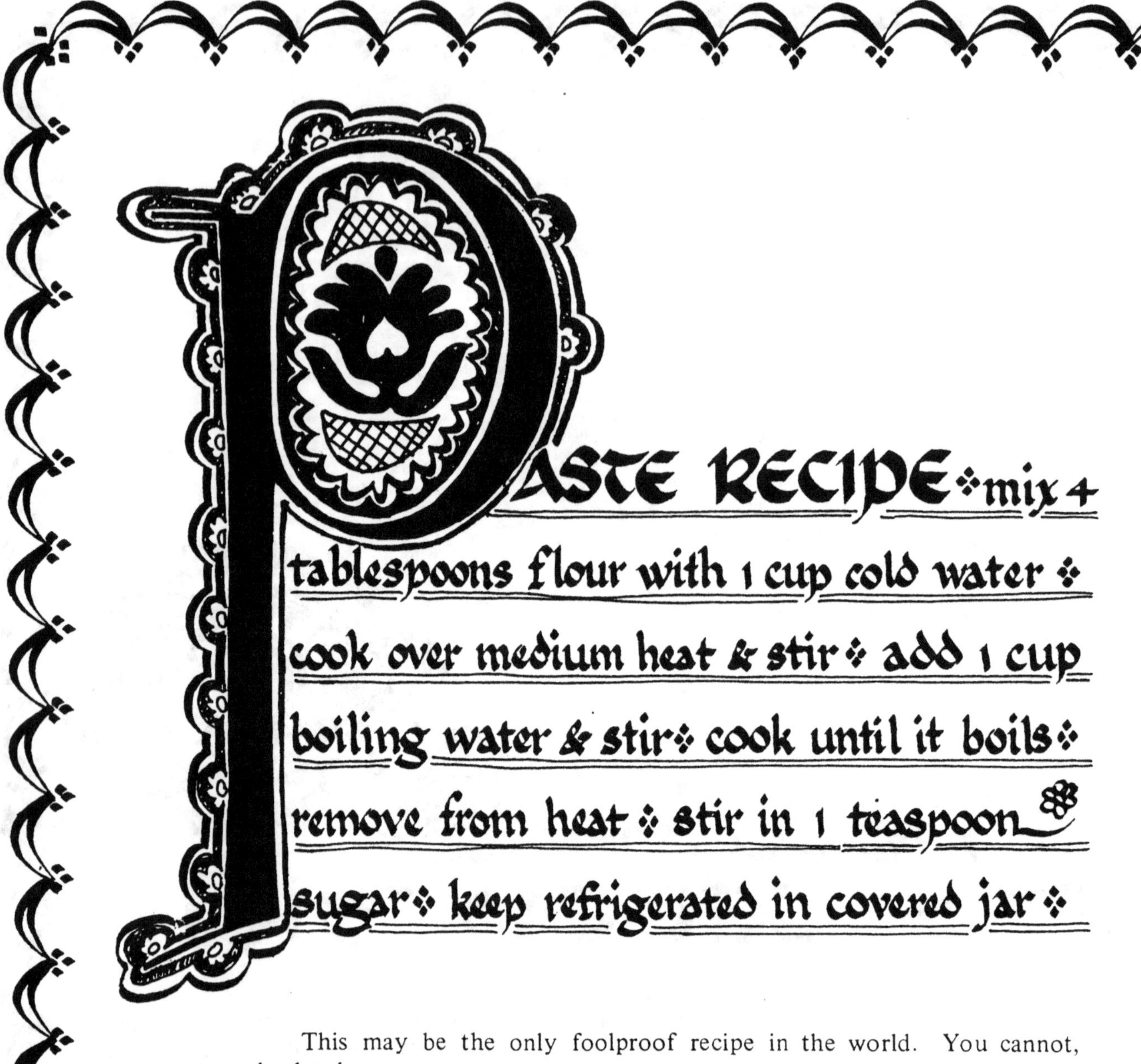

This may be the only foolproof recipe in the world. You cannot, absolutely cannot, go wrong.

1. In a saucepan mix 4 tablespoons flour with 1 cup cold water. One teaspoon of alum may be added for extra cohesiveness but is not necessary.

2. Cook over medium heat, stirring constantly. You can use an egg-beater if the flour is lumpy. Cook until mixture is just below the boil.

3. Add one cup of boiling water. This will cause the mixture to thicken fast.

4. When paste boils, remove from flame.

5. Add 1 teaspoon sugar which gives a fixative quality. You may add at this time a drop or two of oil of cloves. This gives a pleasant aroma to the paste but does not affect the consistency.

Keep paste in a covered jar in the refrigerator where it should last several weeks. When disposing of old paste (in time it will get moldy) wash it down the drain with water to prevent clogging. The paste can be used hot or cold and will work if it's thick or thin. After making it by recipe several times, you'll probably relax on measuring and realize that the formula works and that the only necessity is to boil the ingredients. It is basically the same process used in making gravy or cream sauce.

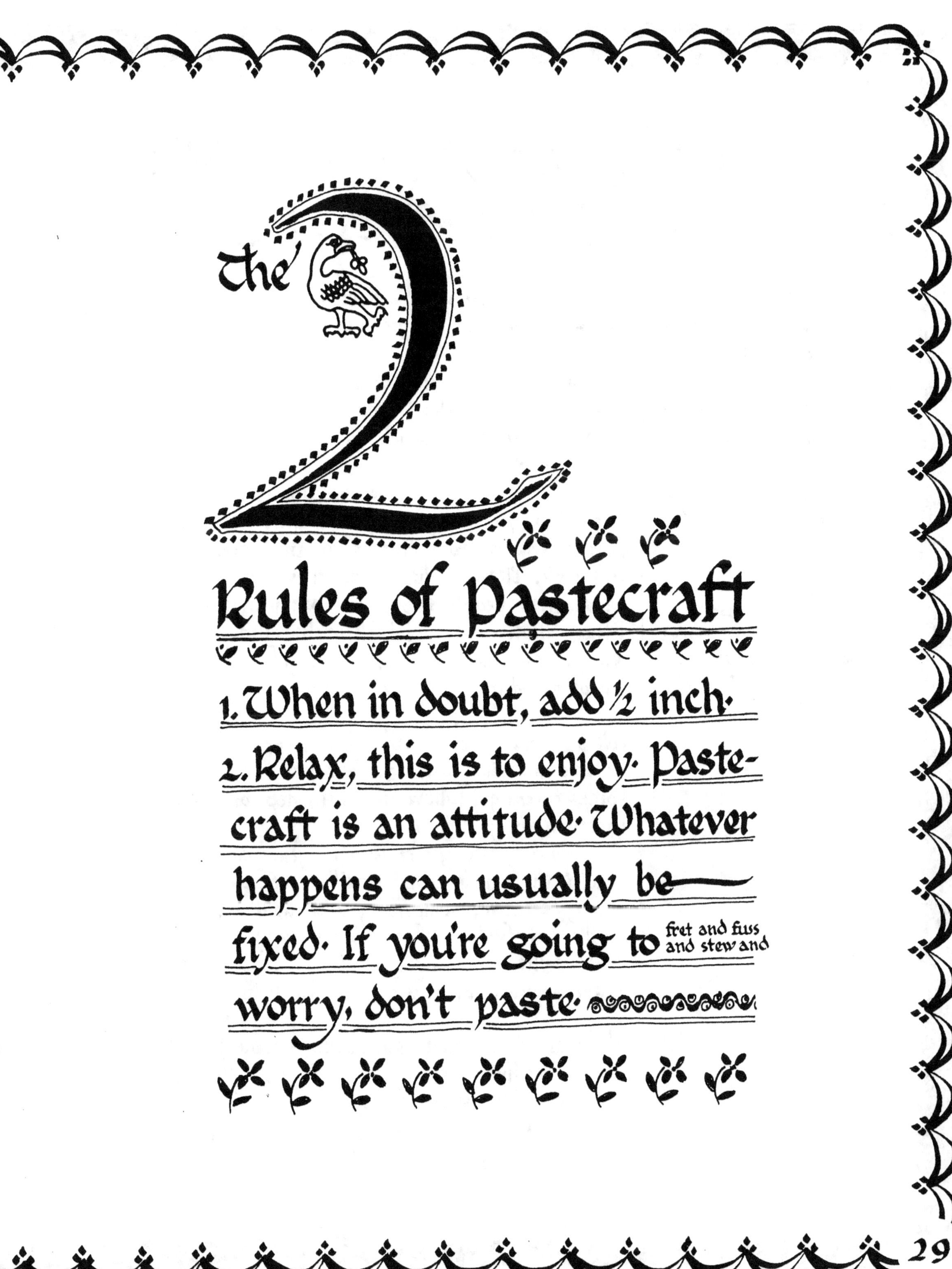

The 2 Rules of Pastecraft

1. When in doubt, add ½ inch.
2. Relax, this is to enjoy. Pastecraft is an attitude. Whatever happens can usually be fixed. If you're going to fret and fuss and stew and worry, don't paste.

O.K. Mary Lou ~ How do I start?

First, declare an hour of your own that will be quiet & uninterrupted. If necessary, close the door & put up a sign to get the point across that this is important to you!

Since everyone needs time to be alone, you are setting an example for those in the household. You may soon observe similar signs on other doors in your home, which can be great fun, as well as a healthy development of self-respect.

POSTED!!
ABSOLUTELY NO INTERRUPTIONS
NO TELEPHONE CALLS
NO VISITORS
NO FIGHTS SETTLED
(KNOCK 3 TIMES IF DESPERATE)
SIGNED Mother

Second, locate a clear table top, put on some of your favorite records & read "Quotes from Pasters", in the back of this book. Please realize that these are sincere words from people like you ~ beginning Pasters. Believe them —— let their thoughts and phrases give you support & strength & inspiration to start on this new endeavor.

Now, roll up your sleeves, cook up some paste & gather the materials listed for the first project, bottle-covering. Follow the easy step-by-step instructions.

Once you're into it, you're on the way & the rest is easy! You'll experience the joy of creating something with your hands & the satisfaction of making a unique beautiful bottle ~ all good feelings. Ideas will start popping of things you want to try.

This is the way Pastecraft stimulates people to use their creativity. The more it is used, the more it grows. The main thing is to get started without being afraid.

Trust me!!! MLC

BEGIN

the
rest
is
easy

Instructions & Ideas

WINE BOTTLE

Covering a bottle is an exercise in basic pastemanship. No talent is necessary, only a positive attitude. Relax, read the directions and have fun. It proves how well fabric sticks to glass, and teaches how to make fabric fit a curve. It is done with 3 pieces of fabric that cover the bottom, sides and lip. It's easy.

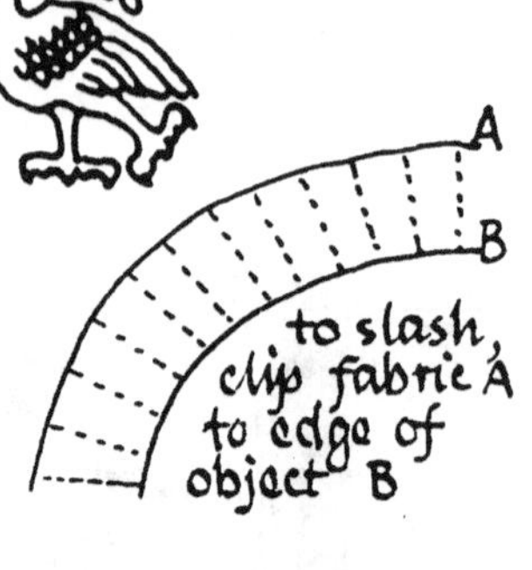

INSTRUCTIONS: Select a tall wine bottle that has nice lines. Soak label off in hot water. Make your paste, choose 1/3 yard (12 inches) of cotton print fabric. Gather brushes, scissors, newspaper, damp towel, soft lead pencil, twine, white glue, shellac, alcohol solvent and you're ready to start.

The first step is to cover the bottom of the bottle. In a corner of the fabric, trace on wrong side a circle 1/2 inch larger than bottom of bottle. Cut out. Lay fabric right side down on newspaper. Brush paste onto wrong side of fabric, making sure that fabric is completely covered with paste. Put wet circle of fabric onto bottom of bottle. Rub fabric until it is well stuck to glass at bottom. Now, to make the protruding 1/2 inch fit over the bottom edge, cut straight slashes 1/2 inch apart, which produces little flaps that are then overlapped one at a time, and pushed firmly over the edge to the sides of the bottle.

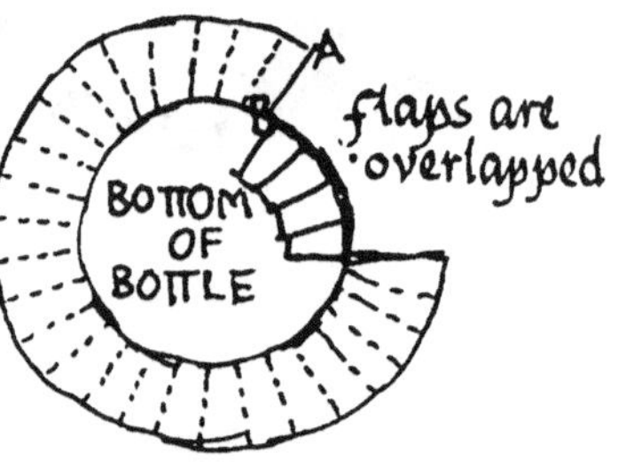

If the bottom of the bottle is indented, cut a circle of cardboard that is 1/8 inch smaller than bottom. Glue onto glass, press, let dry, then cover with fabric.

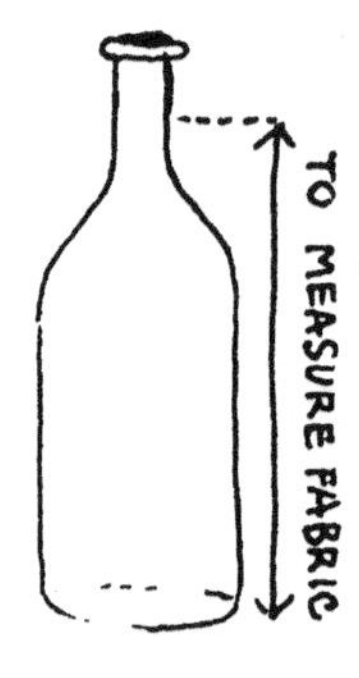

The second step is to measure fabric for the sides, from the bottom edge up to the middle of the bottle neck. Allow 1/2 inch extra around the circumference. If fabric tears easily on the straight of the weave, you will find this is fast and accurate. Apply paste to wrong side of fabric and roll bottle so that fabric clings to it. Starting at center, smooth fabric with hands, getting bubbles and wrinkles out. If a portion of fabric isn't sticking, brush with paste on right side, pushing flat until perfectly smooth. To make fabric fit curve at neck of bottle, cut straight slashes 1/2 inch apart. Pull firmly, overlap and smooth.

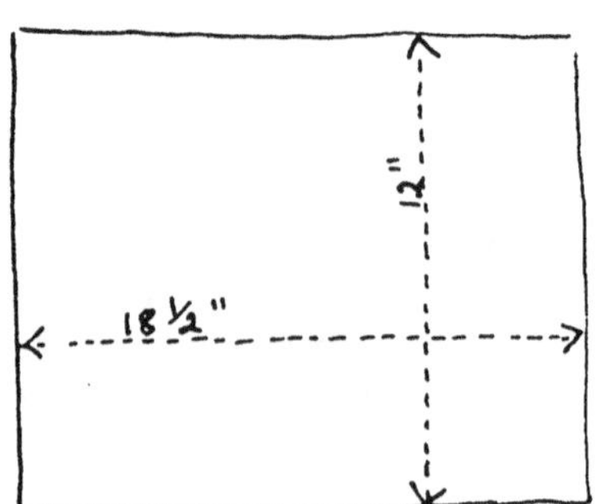

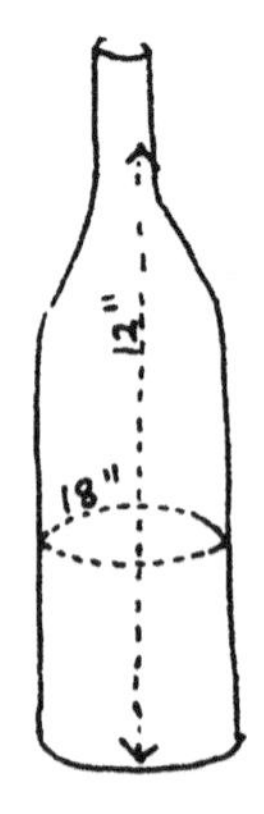

The third step is to cover the lip of the bottle. Tear or cut strips of fabric 1/2 inch wide and 2 inches long. Apply paste and position each strip so that it extends down the neck an inch both inside and out, overlapping until lip is covered.

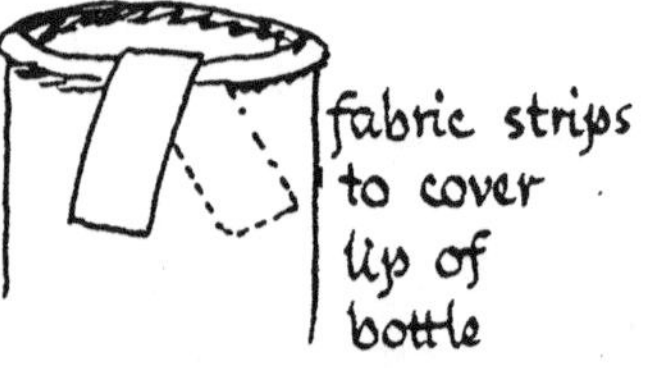

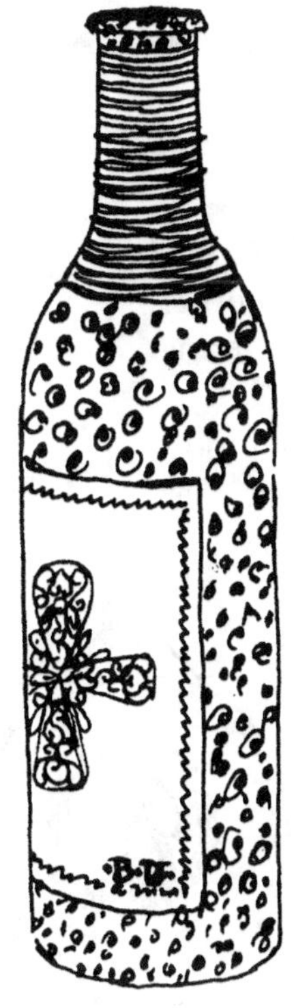

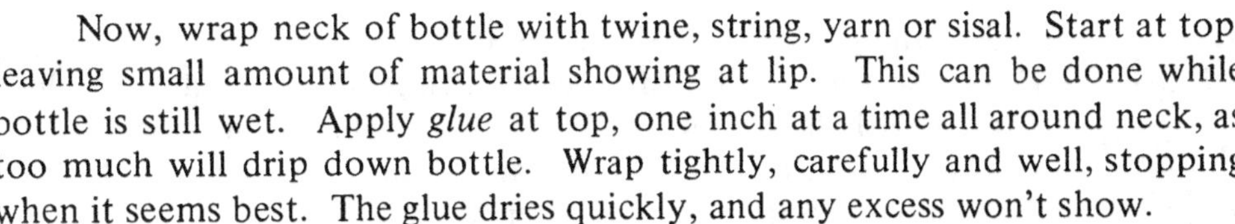

Now, wrap neck of bottle with twine, string, yarn or sisal. Start at top, leaving small amount of material showing at lip. This can be done while bottle is still wet. Apply *glue* at top, one inch at a time all around neck, as too much will drip down bottle. Wrap tightly, carefully and well, stopping when it seems best. The glue dries quickly, and any excess won't show.

When completed, the fabric should adhere exactly to the line of the bottle. Check to see that all surfaces are smooth and that bubbles are pressed out. If a portion of fabric isn't sticking, brush with paste on right side, pushing flat until perfectly smooth.

A picture may be used on the side of bottle if it looks right with the fabric. Apply with either paste or glue. Trim may be added if you wish. Braid, twine, tape, ribbon or yarn can be used. Apply with glue if thick and heavy; paste if a thin fabric tape. Wipe scissors clean with damp towel.

Make a label on white paper, using ink, with your name, date, name of picture used and artist. Put on the bottom of bottle with glue. Shellac. Follow notes on drying and shellacking. Let dry well between coats. Keep brush moist in alcohol solvent in an empty orange juice can. When finished with shellac brush, clean with paper towel and alcohol solvent, followed by sudsing in warm soapy water.

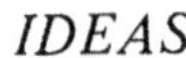

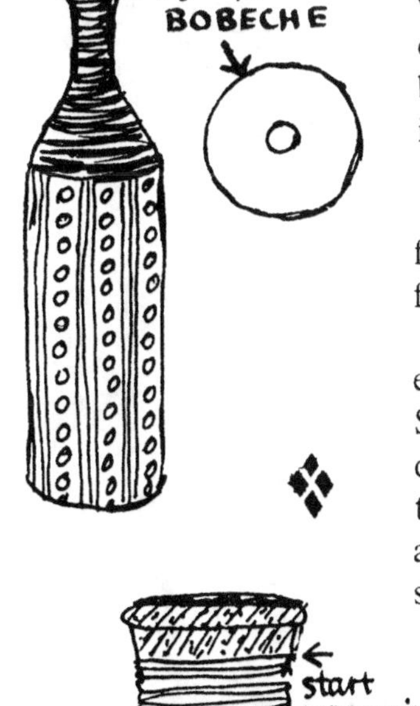

IDEAS

A note on slashing: Slashes are further apart on larger articles such as wastebaskets. Never cut a slash until the fabric is on the object to be covered. How far to slash? As deep as necessary to eliminate puckers. A bottle that has curving sides is difficult to do as it takes too many slashes. It is better in the beginning to work with bottles with fairly straight sides.

Pleased with your first bottle? How about a second, using different fabric? How about teaching and sharing the fun with some kids or a special friend?

For a third bottle try working with velveteen. One precaution, however – use a fresh newspaper so as not to get any paste on front of fabric. Since velvet doesn't slash too well, I usually work with it on the bias (or diagonal), gently pulling and stretching the fabric over the sides of the bottle. Care must be taken not to push the nap down with a fingermark here and there. But do try this as it's beautiful to work with. Velveteen is never shellacked.

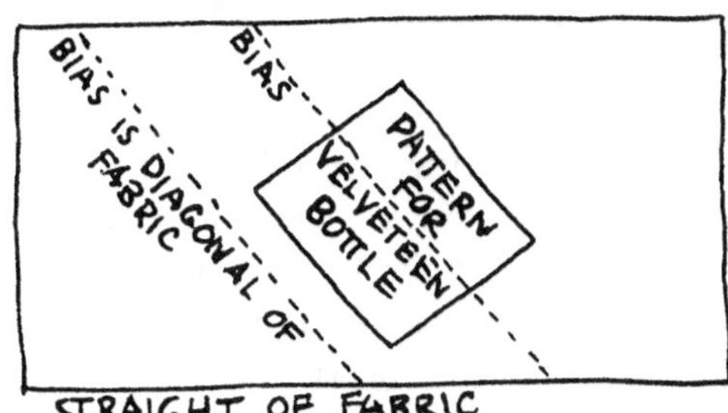

A favorite standby gift of mine is to have several fabric-covered bottles done in advance. Then when a special celebration comes along, I add a handwritten poem, map, drawing or just the name, date and occasion which is

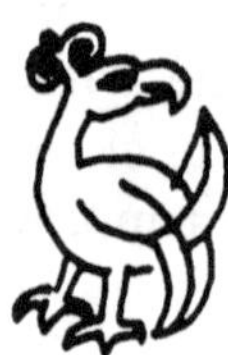

glued on the bottle and sealed with shellac. There's great satisfaction in this kind of thing. A tall bottle makes a nice candleholder, especially if equipped with a bobêche made of several thicknesses of cardboard glued together, covered with fabric and shellacked. A bobêche, in case you're wondering, is a round disc that fits over the candleholder to catch candle drippings.

To use a bottle as a decanter, leave glass tip uncovered inside and out. Fit a cork or decorative stopper in the opening.

SAUCER

This project demonstrates how fabric stretches and covers the curving sides of the saucer without slashing. It makes a beautiful small hanging picture or pincushion.

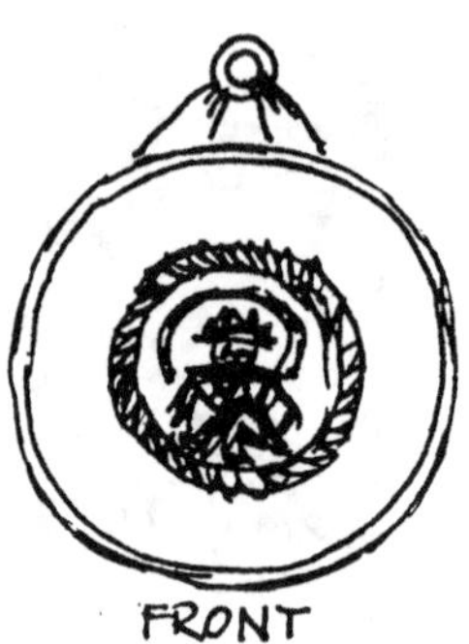

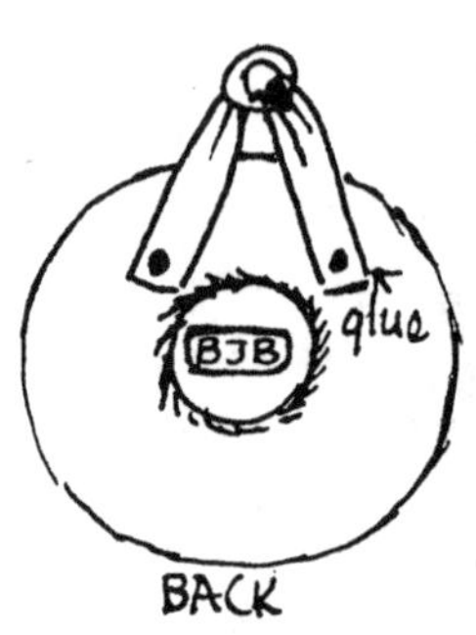

INSTRUCTIONS: You'll need a saucer of any size, either china or plastic, 1/3 yard of fabric, a small piece of thin cardboard, a short piece of ribbon, brass curtain ring, a styrofoam ball 2 1/2 inches in diameter, plus your basic pasting equipment. (See page 18).

To start, mark two circles on back of fabric around edge of saucer, one the exact size, the other 1 inch larger than the saucer. Cut out. Apply paste to back of the larger piece of fabric. Put large circle of wet fabric on front side of saucer, centering it so that the protruding edge is even all around. Rub smooth and make it follow the shape of the saucer perfectly. Because of the shallow shape the fabric will fit smoothly.

Cut slashes 1/2 inch apart in the protruding edge of fabric so that it can be fitted smoothly over edges of saucer. Pull flaps one at a time over edge onto back of saucer where they will overlap each other. Rub until smooth.

Now lay smaller circle of pasted fabric on back of saucer placing it so that it fits saucer well. Rub until smooth. It is not necessary to turn raw edge of fabric under. Rub hard so that it sticks well and it will not show.

To dry saucer, prop it up so that it stands on edge with both sides exposed to the air. When dry, apply shellac to one side, let dry, then apply to other side.

Put a hanger on the back. Make a "V" shaped hanger of a 5 inch length of velvet ribbon or a strip of fabric 1/2 inch wide with edges folded under. String through a brass curtain ring. Apply glue to tips of the "V" and stick to center back of saucer rather than on the slanting sides. This hangs well on the wall and is quite strong.

Put signature label with your name, date, etc., on back.

To make the pincushion, cut styrofoam ball in half with serrated knife. Draw pattern around cut edge of ball on thin cardboard and cut out circle. Attach cardboard to bottom of half ball with 5 straight pins. Draw a large circle on back of fabric and cut out. Do not put paste on fabric. Stretch fabric over curved top of ball, pulling hard over onto back (creases of fabric will show at sides). Fasten edges underneath to cardboard bottom with glue or by pinning through cardboard into ball. Hold tightly until dry, which will take several minutes.

When dry, glue flat side of ball onto center of a fabric covered saucer. Spread glue all over bottom of ball, place in center of saucer, hold down tightly until dry. Trim or braid can be put around edge of ball, using glue. Fabric on the pincushion shouldn't be shellacked.

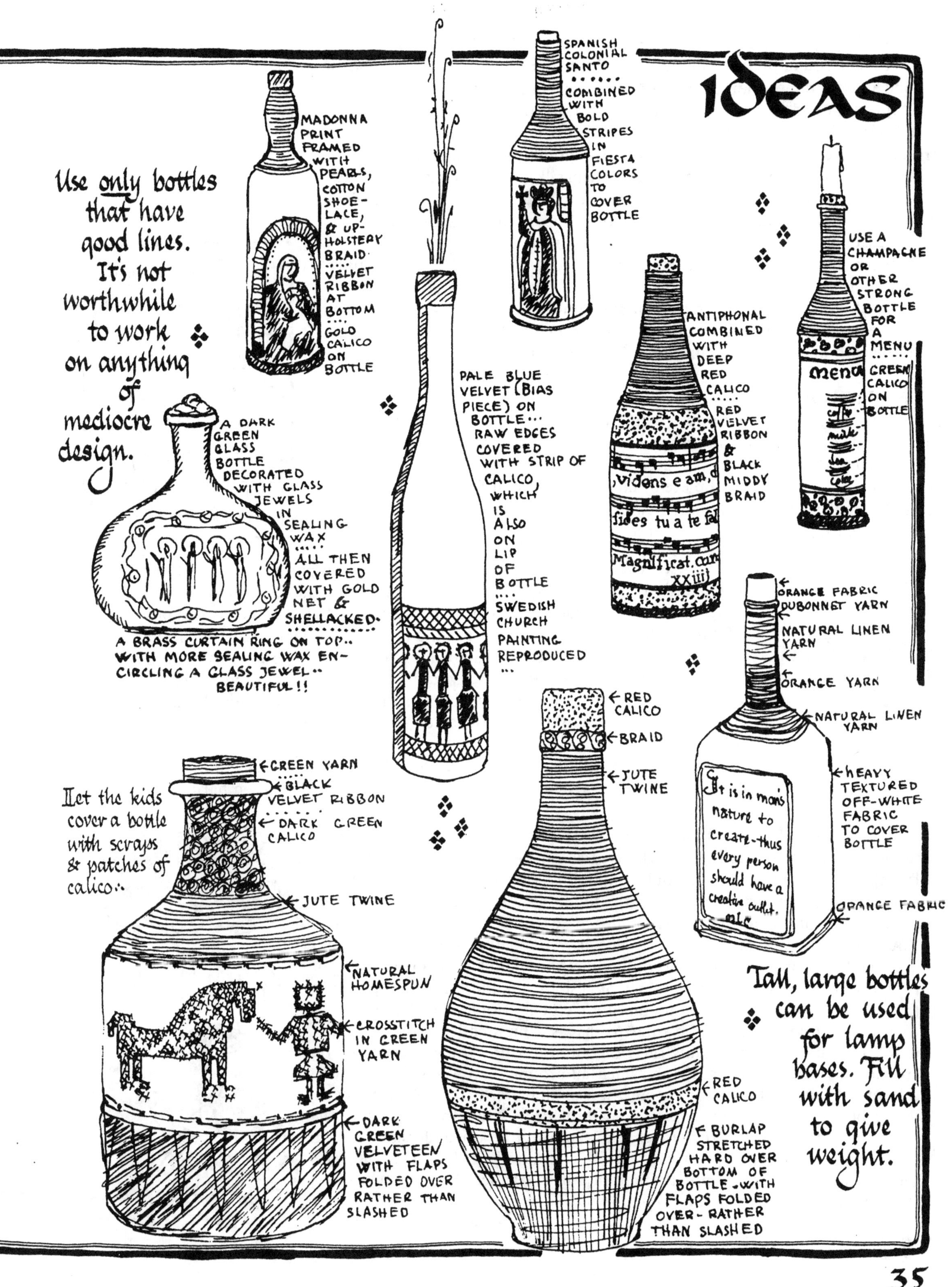
IDEAS
Use only bottles that have good lines. It's not worthwhile to work on anything of mediocre design.
MADONNA PRINT FRAMED WITH PEARLS, COTTON SHOE-LACE, & UP-HOLSTERY BRAID ..... VELVET RIBBON AT BOTTOM .... GOLD CALICO ON BOTTLE
SPANISH COLONIAL SANTO .... COMBINED WITH BOLD STRIPES IN FIESTA COLORS TO COVER BOTTLE
USE A CHAMPAGNE OR OTHER STRONG BOTTLE FOR A MENU ...... GREEN CALICO ON BOTTLE
menu
ANTIPHONAL COMBINED WITH DEEP RED CALICO .... RED VELVET RIBBON & BLACK MIDDY BRAID
,videns e am, d
fides tu a te fa
Magnificat.com
XXiiij
PALE BLUE VELVET (BIAS PIECE) ON BOTTLE... RAW EDGES COVERED WITH STRIP OF CALICO, WHICH IS ALSO ON LIP OF BOTTLE .... SWEDISH CHURCH PAINTING REPRODUCED ...
A DARK GREEN GLASS BOTTLE DECORATED WITH GLASS JEWELS IN SEALING WAX ..... ALL THEN COVERED WITH GOLD NET & SHELLACKED ....
A BRASS CURTAIN RING ON TOP.. WITH MORE SEALING WAX EN-CIRCLING A GLASS JEWEL.. BEAUTIFUL!!
ORANGE FABRIC
DUBONNET YARN
NATURAL LINEN YARN
ORANGE YARN
NATURAL LINEN YARN
HEAVY TEXTURED OFF-WHITE FABRIC TO COVER BOTTLE
It is in man's nature to create-thus every person should have a creative outlet.
ORANGE FABRIC
RED CALICO
BRAID
JUTE TWINE
Let the kids cover a bottle with scraps & patches of calico..
GREEN YARN .... BLACK VELVET RIBBON .... DARK GREEN CALICO
JUTE TWINE
NATURAL HOMESPUN
CROSSTITCH IN GREEN YARN
DARK GREEN VELVETEEN WITH FLAPS FOLDED OVER RATHER THAN SLASHED
RED CALICO
BURLAP STRETCHED HARD OVER BOTTOM OF BOTTLE-WITH FLAPS FOLDED OVER-RATHER THAN SLASHED
Tall, large bottles can be used for lamp bases. Fill with sand to give weight.

IDEAS

A small, round picture can be put in the center of the saucer, with braid around it as a frame, then shellacked for permanence. Sealing wax can also be dripped around the edge for a frame effect. A lovely idea is to use an old watch crystal over a piece of jewelry, setting it in with braid and glue. A group of velveteen saucers can hold grandchildren's pictures. When working with velveteen (cotton velveteen is better than silk), be careful to keep paste and glue away from front side of fabric, as it will spot the pile. A reminder: velveteen is never shellacked. A hand-lettered poem can be set in the saucer and shellacked.

When applying braid, squeeze a line of glue on braid, then carefully press braid where needed. Don't worry about excess drops of glue. When dry it will be transparent. Edges of braid should touch exactly, not overlap. Put an extra dot of glue on both ends and work until dry. Straight ribbon can't be used in trimming a curve, only bias tapes and braids.

> If a BUBBLE shows up after fabric is dry, use a razor blade to cut a slit in the center of bubble. Squeeze enough white glue in so that you can push the fabric completely flat (slit won't show)

TUNA FISH CAN

This project demonstrates pasting on tin and how to cover the inside and outside of a can. A tuna fish can makes a beautiful ring box.

INSTRUCTIONS: You'll need a tuna fish can and lid, washed well, with label removed, a small piece of fabric (trim to match fabric), cardboard (weight similar to laundry shirt boards), foam rubber 1/4 inch thick, and basic pasting equipment.

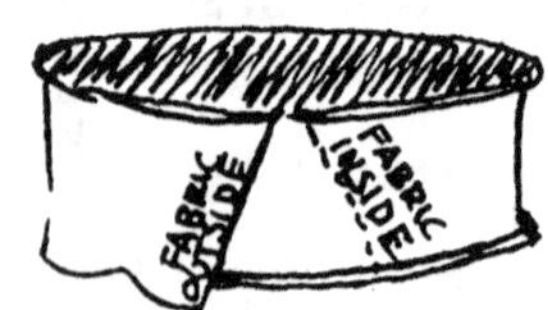

First, cover the sides (inside and out) with one piece of fabric. Cut or tear a strip of fabric twice the height of the side of the can plus 1 inch and long enough to go around the can plus 1/2 inch. Apply paste to this piece of fabric, then fit on the can so that the center of the length goes all around the top rim of the can with the same amount of fabric on outside and inside. It will be messy and wrinkled and you'll wonder if this is going to work. I assure you it will! Start smoothing on the outside and then the inside. You'll have 1/2 inch overlap on the sides. Smooth the seam where the fabric edges overlap.

There is no need to slash where the fabric goes over inside and outside bottoms, as both will be covered, so simply push the folds down hard.

Now, to make a cushion for the inside of can, cut one piece of foam rubber the same size as tin lid. Draw circle on fabric around lid, then add 1 inch extra all around. Cut out. Lay fabric wrong side up on table, put foam circle in center, then tin lid on top. Now drizzle glue (not paste) around edge of tin lid and start pulling the extra inch of fabric over edge. You'll have to work fast before the glue dries. To get a good, tight cushion, keep pulling fabric until it is dry. This method makes a beautiful cushion. Now drizzle more glue on underneath of cushion tin and carefully put inside the can, applying a little pressure until it's stuck. For the underneath bottom of can, draw a circle of cardboard that is a bit smaller than can so that it will fit inside the protruding ridge of can. Cut out. Draw circle on fabric around this cardboard, adding 1/2 inch all around. Now lay fabric wrong side up on table, put circle in center, spread glue around edge of cardboard. Pull fabric over edges gently and hold until dry. This doesn't require the pressure exerted on the tin circle. Now spread glue on underside of cardboard, and put on bottom of can, forcing it inside the ridge. This will warp unless dried correctly, so put the can on a hard surface that moisture won't harm with a heavy weight (brick) on top until dry.

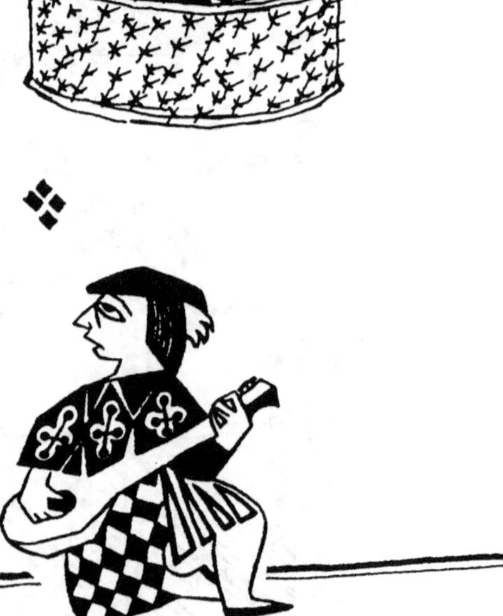

To decorate add ribbon, braid, whatever goes well with the fabric. Measure and cut, glue all along trim, then carefully apply to outside of can. Join edges smoothly. When you have done your best, let it dry, then shellac. The cushioned pad should not be shellacked as it should remain soft and cushiony.

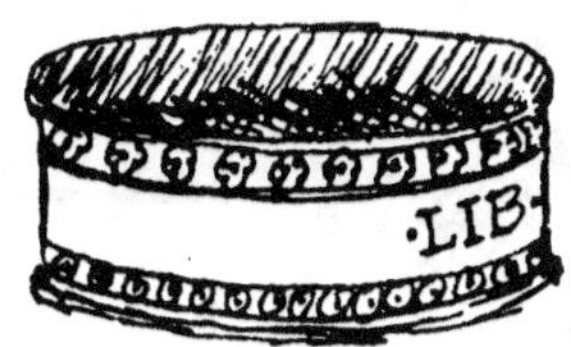

IDEAS

Do you now believe that you can paste on tin? If you ever run into a fabric that for some reason won't hold on tin, my advice is to apply one coat of shellac to the tin and let it dry. The surface will then be rough enough to hold any fabric.

Cans of varied sizes and shapes have infinite possibilities for use, such as holders for pencils, crayons, bobby pins, paper napkins, small toys, paper clips, ad infinitum. Or fill one with homemade candy wrapped in a bit of matching fabric. A velveteen decorated with beads or pearls can be used on the outside to contrast with a print on the inside. This is a super project for children of all ages – Scout troops, school art classes and the housebound.

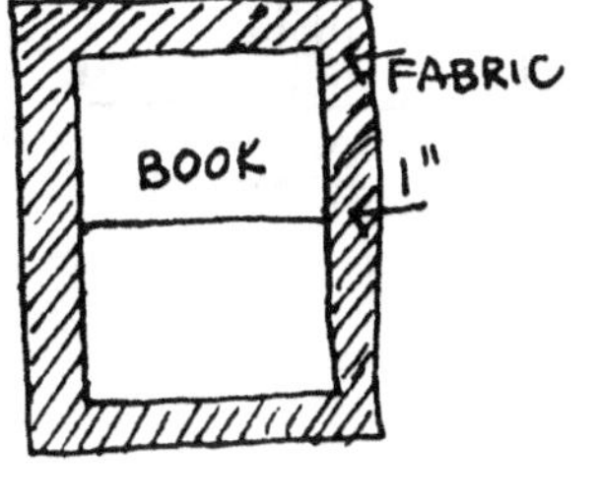

BOOK

The book-covering we are doing is not to be confused with the centuries-old art of bookbinding, although it is one part of the total craft process. It is simple and logical to do, like wrapping a package. The purpose is to give new life to worn-out or dull-looking volumes, to learn how to mend books and to make personal and attractive gifts from blank books, scrapbooks, record books, etc. Note: This process is not intended for hand-bound, leather or fine books, unless they are in very bad condition.

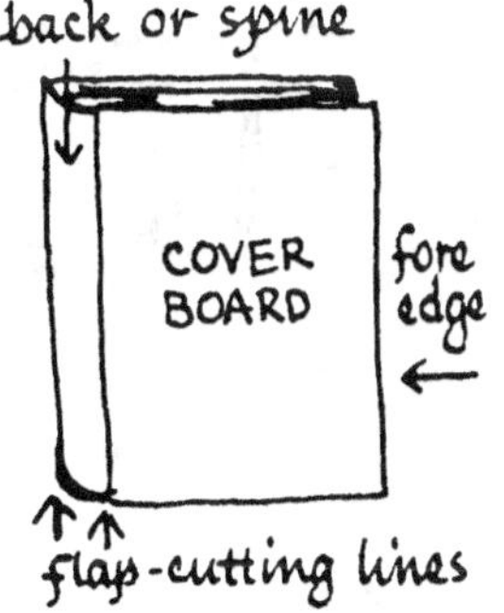

INSTRUCTIONS:

Equipment needed:

Waxed paper.

6 bricks.

Aluminum foil or two pressing plates of thin flat metal, larger than the book. (Plates can be gotten from a sheet metal shop.)

2 pressing boards, 3/4 inch thick, larger than the book, any kind of board.

2 pieces of good paper for end sheets (colored, white, charcoal paper or hand-printed paper).

Heavy rubber band.

First, do all mending and repairing. Mend pages with thin library paste and onionskin paper. Never use Scotch tape, as it will dry, turn brown and stain the pages. Repair back, hinges and covers with glue and muslin strips. A missing cover can be replaced with heavy cardboard or Masonite attached to spine with glue and muslin strips. Paperbacks are given more permanence by gluing heavy cardboard on the outsides.

Fabric should be thick or dark enough so that color and print on original cover won't show through. Linen, light tapestry, brocade, hand-woven fabric, stripes, small prints, velveteen and upholstery fabrics are all good.

To measure fabric, open book at center, lay flat on straight of fabric, cut fabric all around book, allowing one inch extra on all sides.

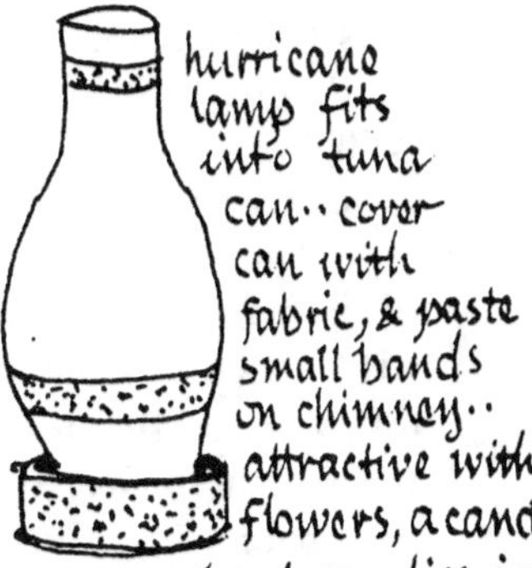

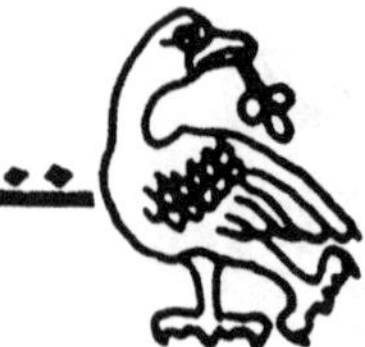

Working on waxed paper (newspaper sticks to fabric when glue is used), lay fabric right side down. To slash at the top and bottom of back, close book, put rubber band around it, and stand on back in center of fabric. Cut two slashes in line with back clear to edge of book, which makes a flap exactly the width of the spine. Put glue on flap and tuck firmly inside hollow back. If it is a tight back and has no tuck-in space, pick up book, fold flap under in line with edge of book, glue to fabric underneath. Let dry.

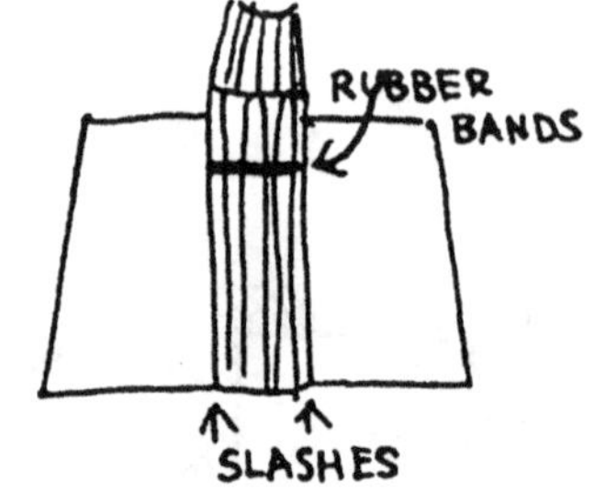

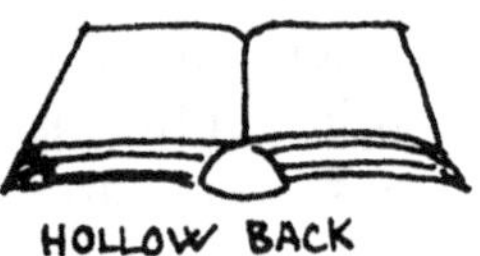

To do first cover, expose one cover, hold rest of book closed tight with rubber band. Prop against firm support so both hands are free. Cut off two corners diagonally (See Mitering a Corner, page 26), leaving space beyond corner the thickness of cover board. Put glue on one flap, pull firmly over edge of cover and rub smooth. Do the same with the other two. Use a bit of glue under fabric at corners, work until neat and flat, making a nice miter. Lay in a piece of aluminum foil or a sheet metal pressing plate over glued area to protect pages. Now close book.

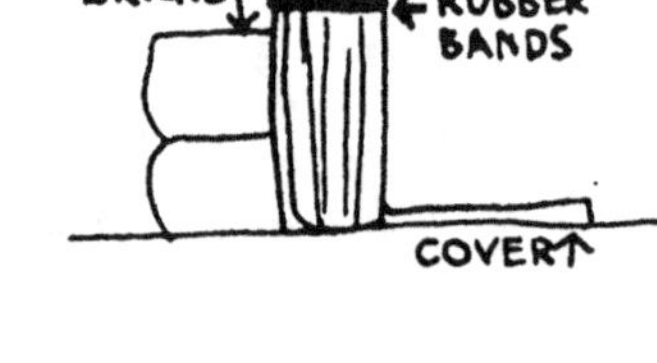

Turn book around and expose other cover, using rubber band to hold rest of book together. Use same procedure as first cover, then lay in pressing plate over glued area. Close book, cover with waxed paper or foil and press with bricks on top until completely dry, at least 24 hours. WARNING: If book isn't allowed to dry completely, it will warp, and you'll have trouble!

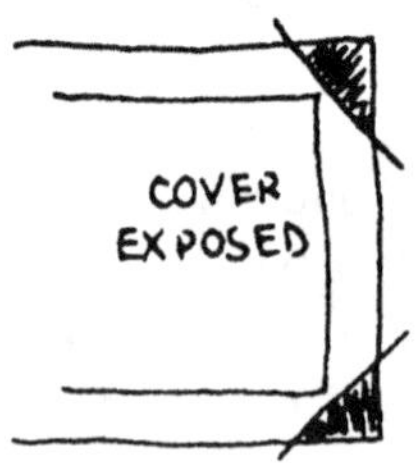

mitering a corner... cut a straight diagonal.. leaving space beyond corner the thickness of board

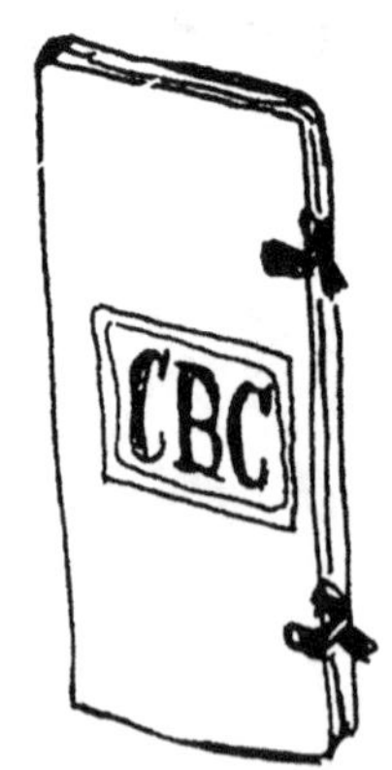

A charming and simple technique is to make ties on the fore edges. This is optional. Though more often used with folios, ties are suitable and handsome with other types of books. They may be made of velvet ribbon, twill tape, shoe strings, leather, etc. They may be placed at middle, top or lower fore edge of cover, or a pair of ties may be used.

The tie is attached to the cover by a slip 1/2 inch from fore edge. The slit is made by hammering a screwdriver completely through the cover board, with an extra piece of wood underneath. Work from the top of cover, then insert tie in slit, leaving two inches inside. Turn book over and hammer flat the rough surface of slit. Glue tie to inside cover. Use foil or pressing plate for protection. Close book and repeat process on other cover.

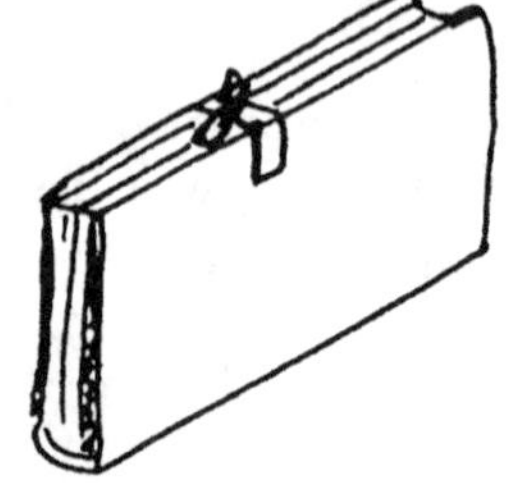

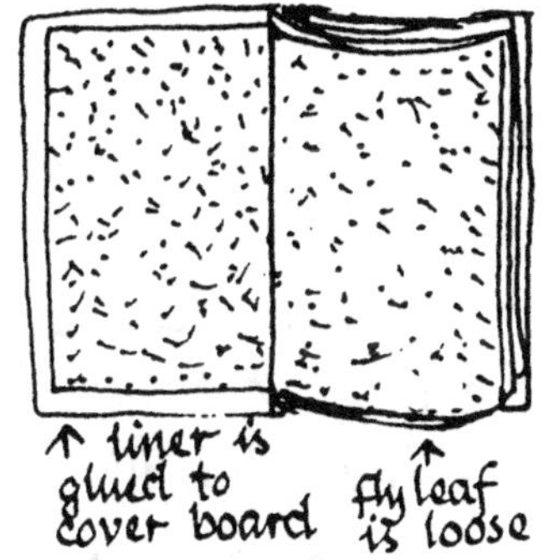

End-Sheets are used inside the front and back covers of a book to give a finished appearance after the cover is done. A variety of papers may be used – marbleized, hand-blocked, heavy white, colored – depending on suitability and relation to the fabric used. It may be a single sheet that is pasted as liner to the inside cover board, or it can be a double sheet, folded so that half of the sheet is pasted to inside cover board as a liner and the other half left free as a flyleaf.

End-sheets are measured the same size as pages of the book, not the cover. To measure, insert end-sheet between pages at center of book, close book, trace with pencil around pages. Then cut carefully. Apply glue in thin line around edges of paper with ample amount on side that will fit into hinge of book. Do not put glue on center part of paper as this will wrinkle and give an uncraftsmanlike appearance. Put end-sheet in place on cover board, about 1/8 inch from all edges of book. Lay in pressing plate, close book, and press until dry.

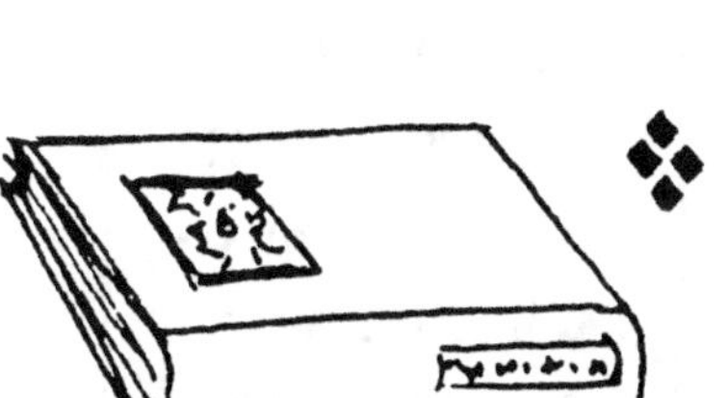

A label must be put on back of book for identification. It can be made from typing paper, charcoal paper, stationery, etc. Use India ink and dip pen to write or print name of book and author. Place carefully on back using glue; rub well. In order to achieve uniformity when doing many books, place labels two inches from bottom of book. A larger and more decorative label may be put on front cover, or an appropriate picture may be used.

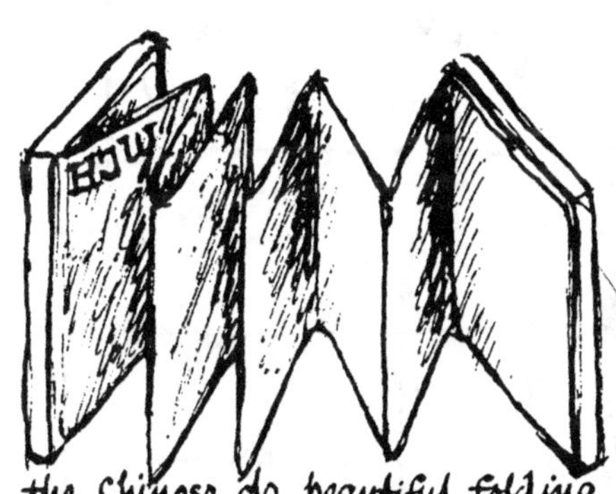

the Chinese do beautiful folding books. covers are made of masonite or plywood. long pieces of paper are carefully glued together and folded in accordion fashion. can be used for photo album, poetry, guest books, notes, etcetera.......

IDEAS

This technique of using glue for book-covering is fast and simple. As you will notice, all glue will be on inside of the covers for neat appearance. Should you want fabric to be completely pasted to book covers, use paste applied to total fabric which must be pressed under heavy weight until completely dry to keep cover boards from warping.

Through the years I've covered worn-out or uninteresting books in a variety of calicos, which has added an effective and personal touch to our library. Books should not be shellacked.

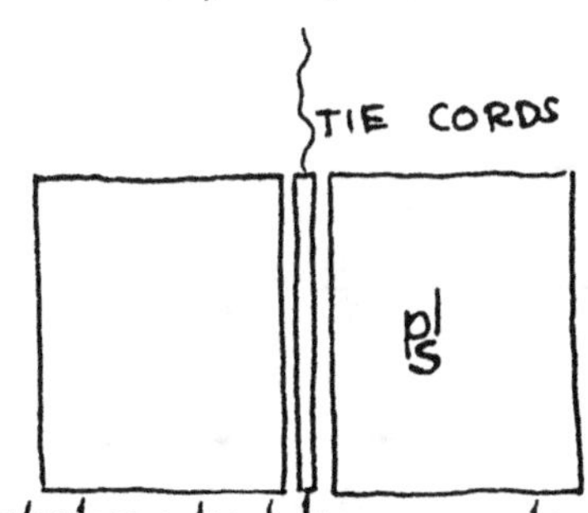

telephone book cover made from masonite or heavy cardboard.. center piece is thickness of book.. lay 3 pieces on heavy fabric & cover while flat..

Different kinds of books can be tried: Folios, notebooks, accordion fold. To make a padded book, put foam rubber underneath fabric on the book cover. Treasure Gold may be rubbed on tightly-held page edges as finish for special book.

Decorative covers and different media used in centuries past give ideas for creative methods. The beautiful "table books" were covered with embroidery, pierced metal, carved ivory and wood, velvet, appliqué, and often closed with metal clasps. Some were embellished with gold tooling, metals, jewels, leather inlay, etc.

Hand-decorated end-sheets can be made with simple block-printing media such as potatoes, erasers or linoleum.

BLOCK OF WOOD

It's time to learn the simple, basic technique of covering corners of a thick board, which can later be applied to various projects. It is important that a corner be covered well.

INSTRUCTIONS: Cut or tear enough fabric to go over the sides and several inches onto the back of board. Apply paste to fabric; lay board in center of fabric.

1. Cut 4 slashes in straight line with board.
2. Cut slash the thickness of side of board.
3. Cut out corners (*2-3*), in straight line with board.
4. Pull 2 sides over to back.
5. Pull 4 tabs (*1-2*) around corners, covering ends of board.
6. Pull last 2 sides tightly over to back.

An easy way to cover a corner is to cut corners out of fabric. Then use this corner piece to cut a strip that is the exact width of the side of board. Apply paste and put the patch over the corner. Then pull the four flaps up tight over to back.

IDEAS

Make a tray, using a piece of 5-ply wood, 9 x 18 inches. Paste fabric, put on board, shellac. Then screw brass or black iron window pulls at each end for handles. Make several napkins of same fabric to match.

If your fabric is WRINKLED before working on it, it's not necessary to iron it. When paste is applied, you'll discover that the moisture makes the fabric limp, wet & heavy.

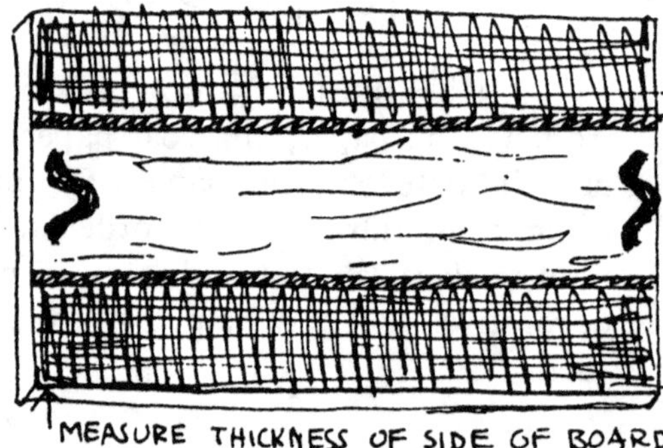

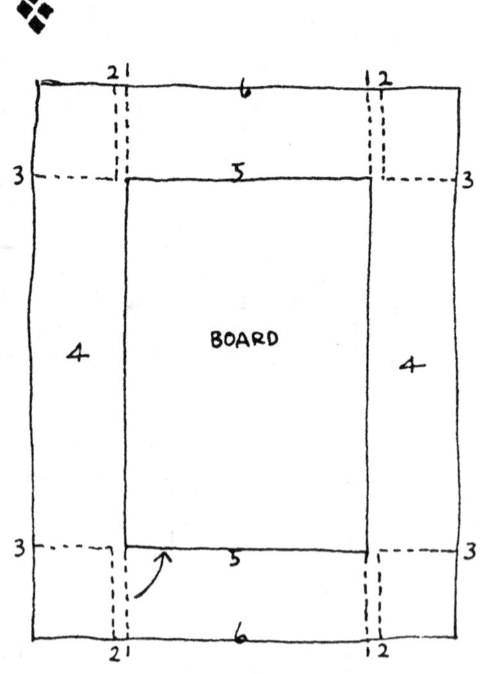

TABLETOPS

Don't toss out that table with the irreparable surface. The possibilities for reclaiming it by covering it with fabric are exciting. Wonderfully effective things can be done. No matter if you've never seen one like it, if it sounds good to you, go ahead.

Be sure that the table is structurally sound, firm and of the right height. If you need a coffee table and don't have the right size, visit a secondhand store where, with imagination, you can probably find something.

You can make a table from a plank door mounted on four sturdy legs or think about reviving an old bridge table, coffee table, dining room table, kitchen table or dressing table.

INSTRUCTIONS: See that the table surface is smooth. Fill small cracks, dents, scratches with glue. When dry, sandpaper until smooth and level. Fill large holes with torn strips of newspaper soaked in paste. Push down firmly and allow to dry thoroughly. Also sand this surface until smooth.

To measure fabric for tabletop, allow enough to go over the edge and underneath for two inches. If table has ridges or beveled edge, allow more fabric and see that fabric follows these interesting lines. Paste fabric, place on tabletop, smooth, miter the corners, let dry and shellac heavily. Wax if you wish for extra finish. Paint table legs a color that enhances and goes with the fabric.

Home decorating ideas using board-covering technique

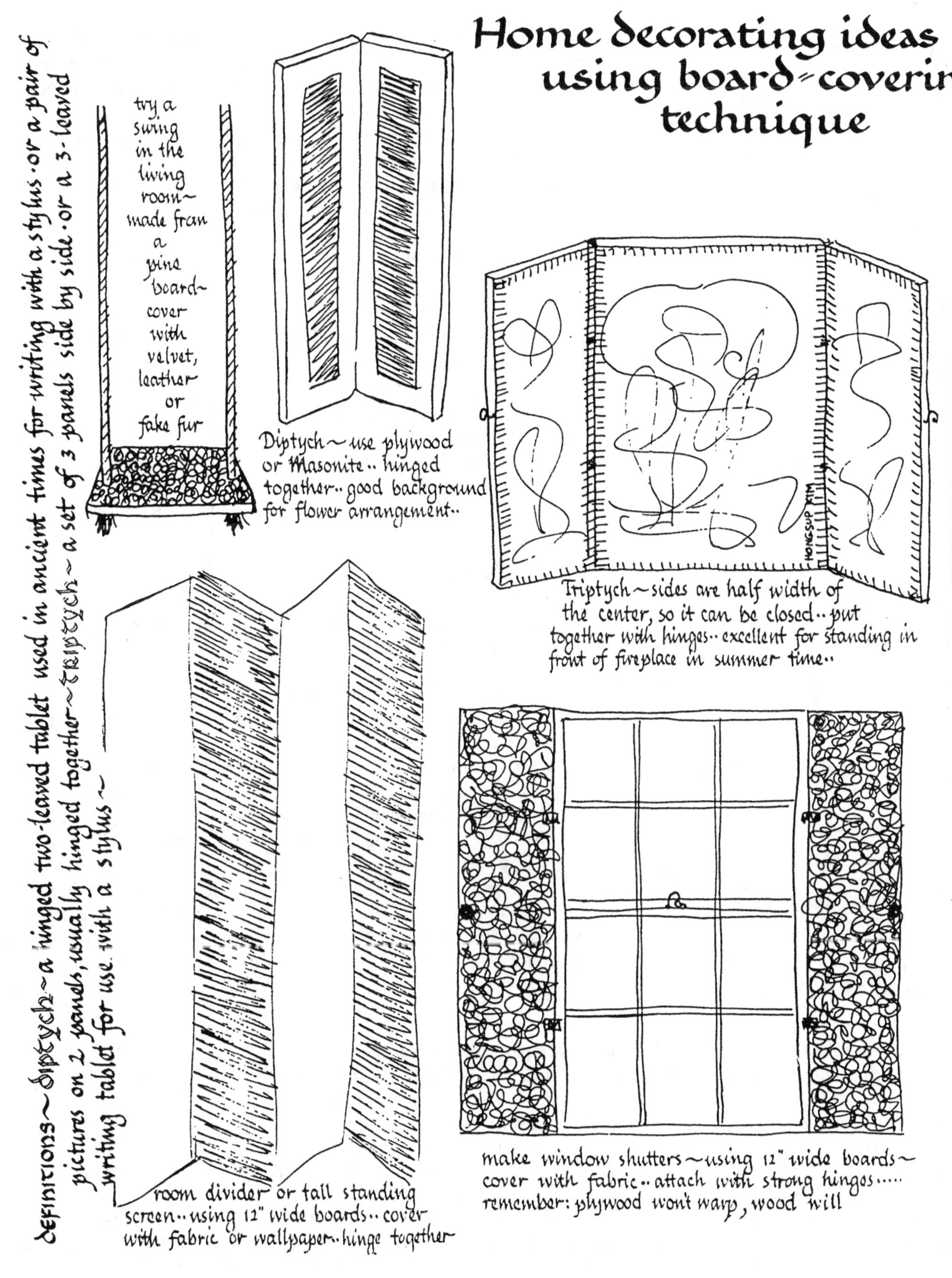

try a swing in the living room ~ made from a pine board ~ cover with velvet, leather or fake fur

Diptych ~ use plywood or Masonite .. hinged together .. good background for flower arrangement ..

Triptych ~ sides are half width of the center, so it can be closed .. put together with hinges .. excellent for standing in front of fireplace in summer time ..

room divider or tall standing screen .. using 12" wide boards .. cover with fabric or wallpaper .. hinge together

make window shutters ~ using 12" wide boards ~ cover with fabric .. attach with strong hinges ..... remember: plywood won't warp, wood will

definitions ~ diptych ~ a hinged two-leaved tablet used in ancient times for writing with a stylus · or a pair of pictures on 2 panels, usually hinged together ~ triptych ~ a set of 3 panels side by side · or a 3-leaved writing tablet for use with a stylus ~

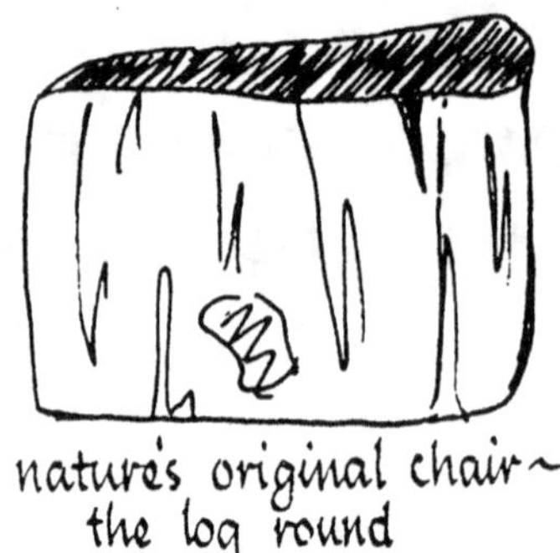
nature's original chair~ the log round

IDEAS

You might center a coffee table with an old map, framed with braid, or burn the edges with a candle for an antique finish. Use drawings that the children have done. You can have a piece of glass cut the exact size of the table at a hardware store.

A set of log rounds placed around a low table and shellacked are great for stools. Make cushions of foam rubber and cover with matching fabric. To prepare chairs to go with your new table, paint everything except the seat, cover the seat with fabric, shellac, and make a cushion covered with the same fabric. Or, you might do a bench to pull up to the dining table. Cover the board with fabric, shellac and make a matching cushion.

PICTURE FRAMES

Framing a picture without a frame is a neat and simple technique that may be the most valuable technique in this book! Choose a small picture (for example one 5 x 7), a wedding announcement or postcard reproduction. Then select a fabric for framing this, a fabric that goes well with the particular picture or card. Use cotton, velveteen, corduroy or heavy linen. It is important to consider the total effect, as the combination of picture and fabric must be right. The decorative border or ornamental finishing strip should enhance, but not overpower, the picture. A small geometric print may be used with discretion and deliberate care.

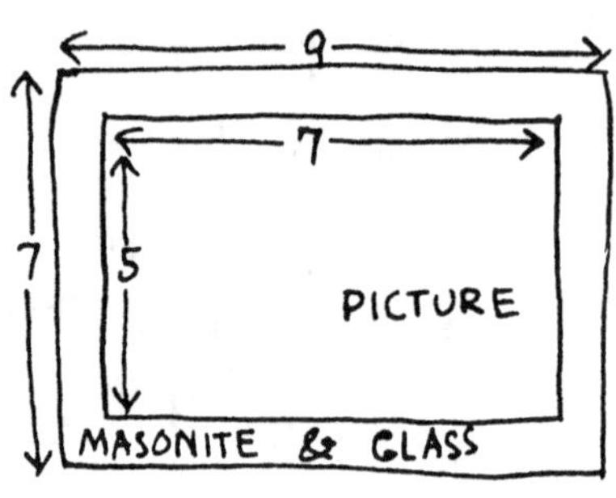

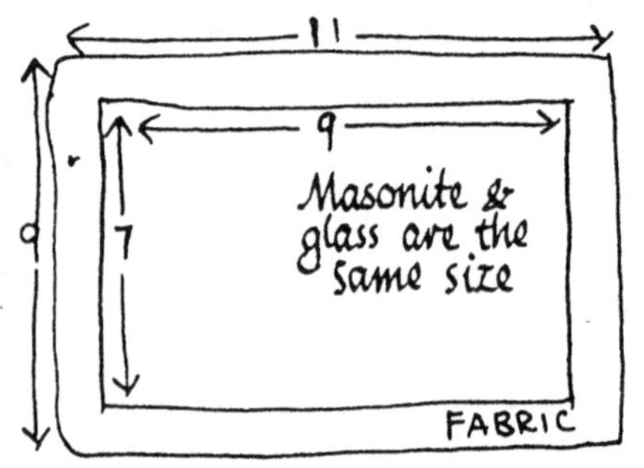

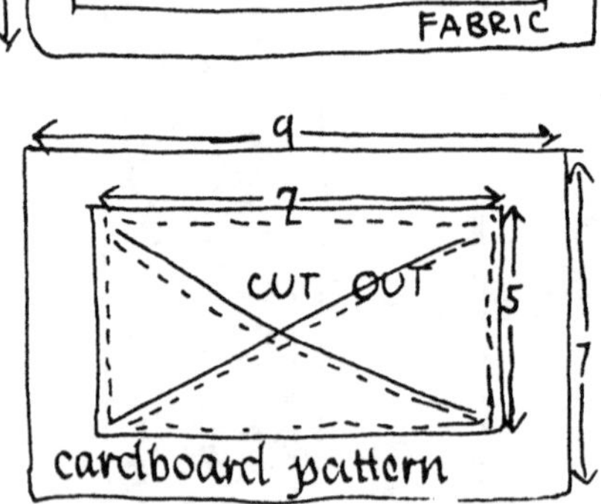

INSTRUCTIONS:

Materials:

- Piece of glass (any thickness) larger than picture.
- Piece of Masonite or plywood (any thickness) the same size as glass.
- Mat board from art supply store.
- Brown kraft paper for backing (or grocery store paper bag).
- Brass curtain ring.
- Utility knife with razor blade insert, Exacto.
- Metal-edged ruler.
- Plus basic equipment (page 24).

NOTE: The glass, Masonite and mat board are all to be the same size; which is larger than the picture, from 1/2 inch border to several inches on all sides. This is an arbitrary decision.

Now cut or tear fabric one inch larger on all sides than picture. Measure picture placement in exact center of Masonite, and mark lines with pencil. Run a thin line of glue around inside edge of pencil line (no glue in center, it may wrinkle and ruin picture). Place picture inside marked lines.

Clean glass well on both sides with vinegar. Put large dot of glue in each corner of Masonite and put glass on this; use wooden clothes pins at edges to hold together while drying. Check to see that picture is placed accurately and edges of glass and Masonite are even.

Now, to make the cardboard pattern that is the essence of this process, mark with pencil the exact size of picture (5 x 7) in center of mat board. Cut this out with Exacto knife. Test over picture to see if it fits correctly.

Lay this cardboard pattern onto back of fabric after applying small dots of glue at corners to hold fabric. Let dry. Now cut out fabric in center. Slash to each corner, leave 1/2 inch inside cardboard pattern, cut all the rest away. Then run glue on back side of these flaps of fabric edge and turn

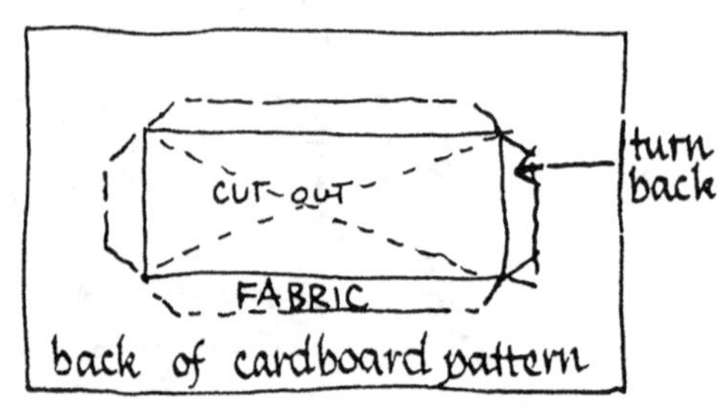

back of cardboard pattern

back onto cardboard pattern. Let dry. Then run glue on back side of pattern, and put on glass in proper place to frame picture. Let dry.

Turn over. You'll be pleased with the effect you have. Now pull extra fabric over onto back of Masonite, using technique you learned in covering the block of wood and using glue.

To make hanger, mark center back, use ribbon or strip of calico, put through brass ring. Glue in triangular shape at top barely above edge of picture. Backing paper is used to cover the raw edges and give a finished appearance. Mark the brown kraft paper 1/4 inch smaller on all sides than Masonite. Cut out, then run glue around edges or brush paste all over, which shrinks the paper and gives a great fit.

Letter or write on the back the name of picture, artist, date and your signature.

design a shape for framing picture by cutting a piece of folded paper—so both sides match

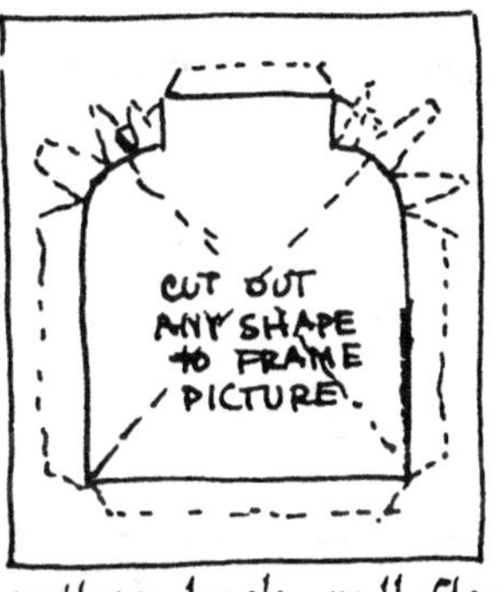

pattern back..pull flaps of fabric onto back.... glue to cardboard...

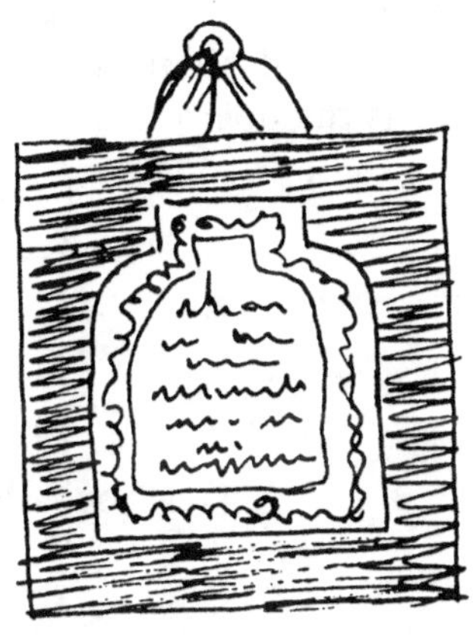

NOTE: There are two methods of framing a picture. First, the cardboard pattern or single-piece described above, and second, the strip or four-piece process. The single-piece method is used when working with heavy fabrics, such as velvet, corduroy, upholstery fabric, etc. The four-piece process is used when working with lightweight cotton prints.

The second method is easy. Follow same steps as the pattern method so that glass is glued onto Masonite. Dry before next step.

Cut four strips of fabric two inches wide and about seven inches long. Put paste on back of strips. Then carefully lay fabric strips one at a time onto glass to edge of picture, making a fabric border. Corners can be mitered and excess fabric pulled over to the back, where it is pressed down. Make hanging ring same as in first method, then add brown kraft paper on back and signature.

Use narrow ribbon, braid, or dripped sealing wax to cover raw edges of fabric and, also, to provide a three-dimensional frame for picture.

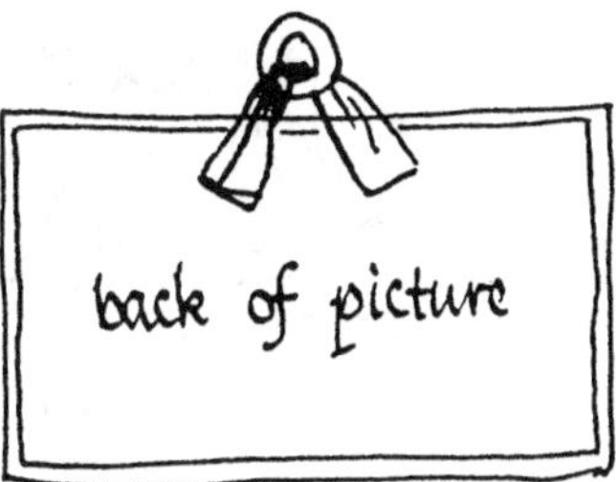

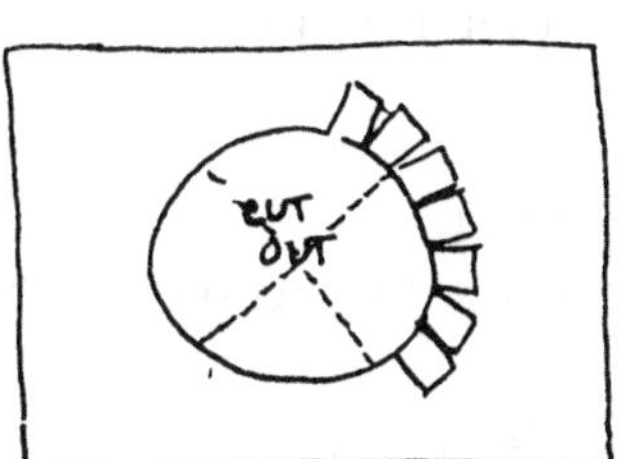

back of round cardboard pattern..pull flaps of fabric onto back..glue to cardboard

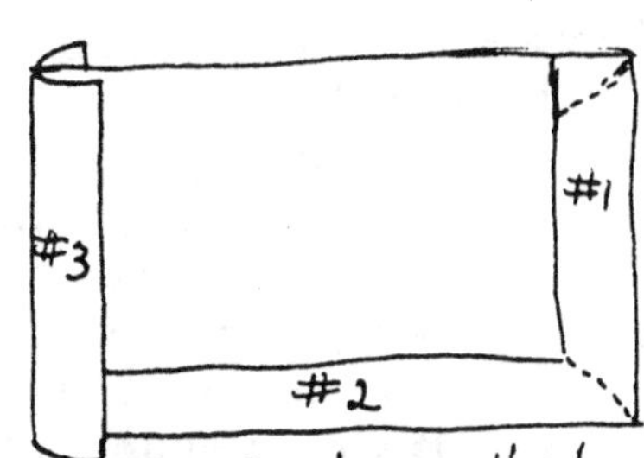

4-strips framing method... each piece goes over front & back.. cut corners on the diagonal..

IDEAS

When doing a group of pictures, you can achieve unity by covering all frames in same fabric and hanging close together. Or use several calicos or velveteen for contrast. Wooden frames may also be covered, with attention to good mitering jobs.

For the special effect of a padded frame, especially when using velveteen, put strips of foam rubber underneath fabric. Be careful never to allow moisture to touch picture. Never use Scotch tape on valuable pictures as it is injurious to good paper and turns brown. For dimensional effect, cover a larger board with fabric, then glue smaller framed picture in center. Put together with the super-stick method (page 51).

If framing a page from an old book, and you want both sides to show, use two pieces of glass held together with a strip of fabric or ribbon over the edges. Slip ribbon hanger in between the two glasses – all of this applied with glue for strength.

Remember, the Masonite back is bigger than the picture, and the glass is the same size as the board. The rest is easy.

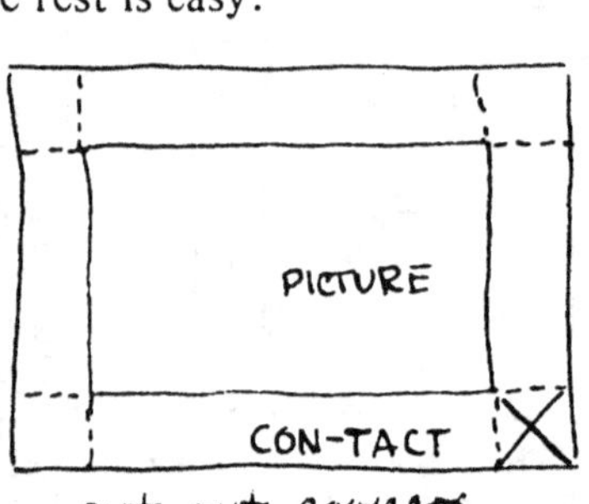

cut out corners

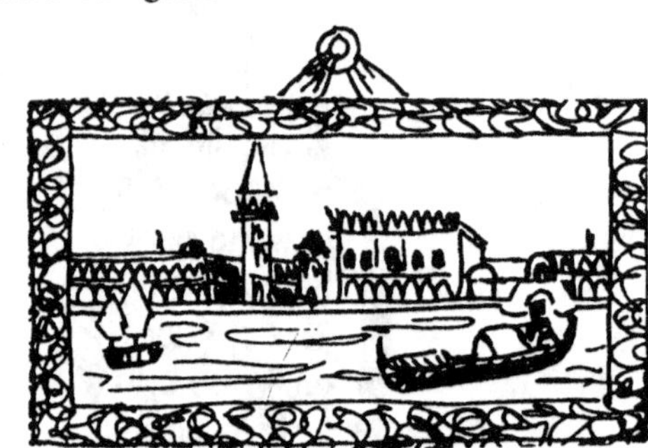

SUPER-SIMPLE PICTURE FRAMING WITHOUT GLASS

This is a method using clear Con-tact paper that is good for small pictures, prints and certificates that need to be protected and preserved.

Cut cardboard or poster board the same size as the picture. Then cut a piece of Con-tact several inches larger than picture, so that at least an inch of Con-tact can go over onto back. Pull paper off back of Con-tact and place flat on worktable. Press front of picture down in center of Con-tact, then put dots of glue in corners of picture and press cardboard in place. Rub and smooth to get wrinkles out. Then cut corners off Con-tact in line with sides of picture. Pull each strip over onto back. Make ribbon hanger and cover back with brown kraft paper.

LAMPSHADE

This section tells how to revitalize lampshades that are worn or the wrong color. It's easy to do, will save money (check with any decorator as to the cost of custom lampshades), and helps coordinate accessories in a certain room. This is one of the few times that wallpaper can be used, as there are no curves to fit, no slashes needed, therefore no fear of tearing.

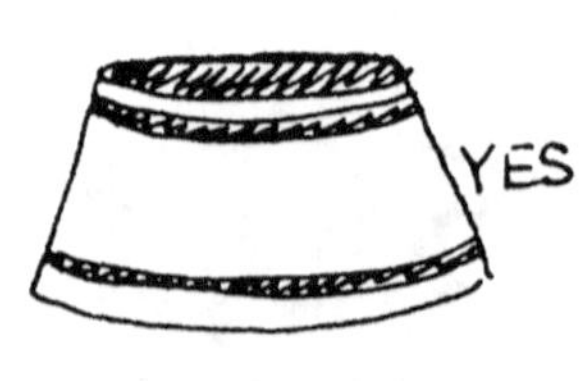

INSTRUCTIONS:

Materials:

- Lampshade of parchment, cardboard, fabric, etc.
- 1/2 to 1 yard fabric or wallpaper, according to size of shade.
- Several yards cotton bias tape for trim.
- Wooden clothes pins to use in drying.
- Plus basic equipment (page 24).

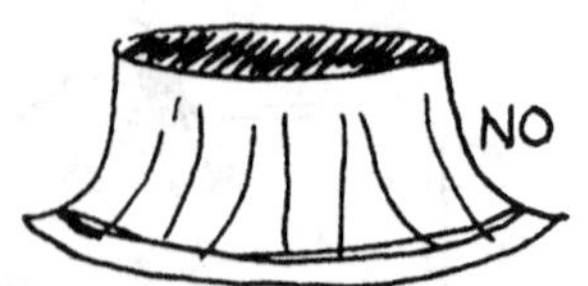

Basic shape is the first consideration in covering a lampshade. You can't cover a shade that curves inward, outward or is gathered. The sides of

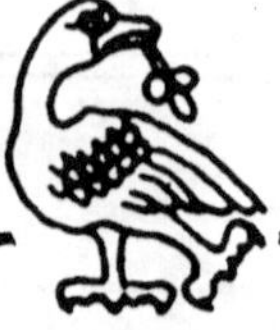

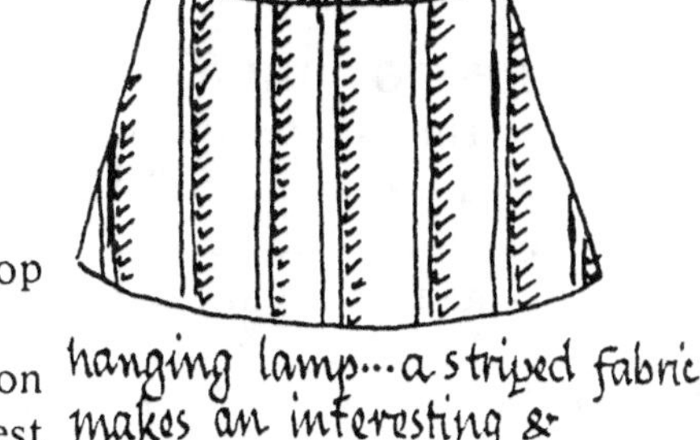

hanging lamp...a striped fabric makes an interesting & decorative shade...

the shade must be straight and constructed with strong metal wires at top and bottom.

There must be enough fabric to wrap once around the shade, either on the straight of the fabric or the bias (diagonal). It is also necessary to test shade over lighted lamp with new fabric held over it to see if any of the design or color underneath shows through. If it does, select a darker or heavier fabric or wallpaper.

Now take shade off lamp. If shade needs repair of rusted metal wire or has too dark a color for the new fabric, cover these problems with light-colored cotton bias tape, or a bias strip of sheeting applied with glue. Let all mending dry before proceeding with next step.

Draw a pattern of the shade on newspaper with soft lead pencil. If the shade is large, tape several papers together. Lay the shade down on the paper, and locate the vertical seam in lampshade. Mark this seam on paper pattern at top and bottom and slowly roll shade around to starting point, marking as you go. If you lose your place, start over. Allow 1/2 inch overlap at one side when marking. Cut pattern from paper, making top and bottom edges a bit smaller than the shade to fit just inside metal rings.

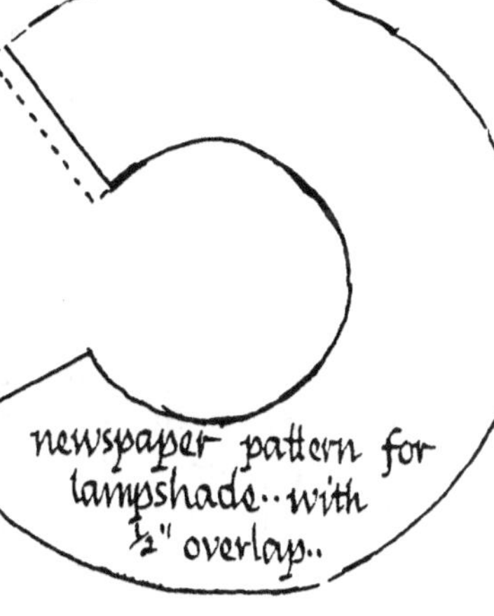

newspaper pattern for lampshade..with ½" overlap..

Lay fabric wrong side up, trace with pencil or chalk around pattern, then cut out. Now lay fabric on newspapers and apply paste. Lay lampshade in center of wet fabric and bring up on both sides. Slowly work fabric around until it fits well. Remember, some part of this fabric will be on the bias, so don't pull too hard at any one spot. Make a neat overlap, as it will show when the light is turned on.

Now trim and cover edges, top and bottom. If some edges are too long, simply trim them off even with the shade. This must not be turned over to the other side as it will show. The raw edges must be covered to give a finished appearance. Measure the correct length of bias tape, allowing 1/2 inch overlap. Brush with paste and carefully cover top and bottom edges of shade so that tape extends over both back and front of shade (same method as tuna fish can). Pinch or press tape well for an even and firm finish. Use clothes pins to hold until dry. To dry, put shade on lamp. Do not shellac.

IDEAS

If a plain color is used to cover shade, a beautiful cut-out flower may be pasted on. Silhouettes of leaves, weeds, and dried flowers may be used by pasting these pressed, dried flowers on the original shade before covering. In other words, sandwich them between fabrics.

STRING ON THINGS

This is a technique so useful that it deserves a section of its own. You have already wrapped the bottle neck with jute twine and know that it's easy to do. So here are some practical applications for this technique as a strong repairing method.

First, to mend the handle of a suitcase, strengthen the inside with a piece of leather or rope. If the shape is flat and needs to be built out, pad with cotton or fabric. Then wrap tightly and carefully with jute applied with glue. This can also be used to reinforce a drawer, purse or bag handle.

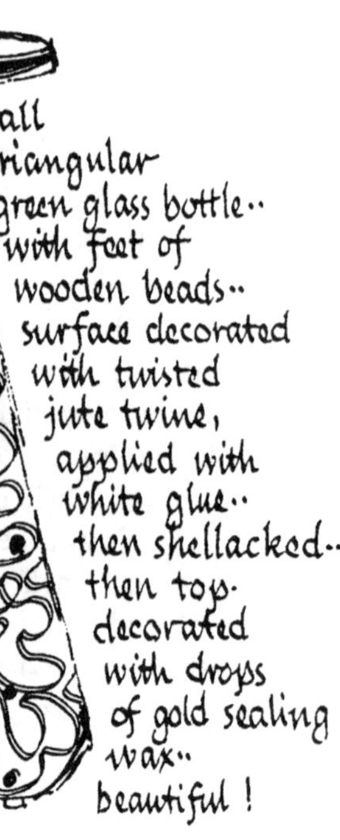

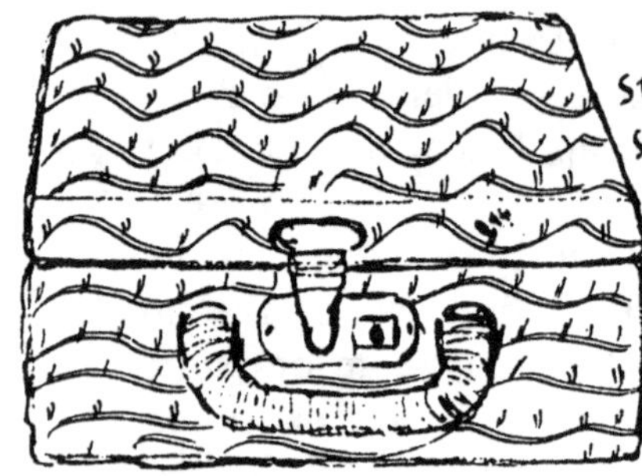

A good way to make a fireplace broom: start with a rough heavy stick, straight or crooked. Then gather broom corn, heavy weeds – whatever grows in your area. Hold around stick and make a temporary wrapping with a strip of fabric. Then wrap with twine and glue. Put braid at each edge.

This process would give a good grip to the car steering wheel. Or wrap a broom handle or dowel with twine to use as a base for a candlestick or a wall hanger for a heavy display rug. Or wrap a huge bottle with twine to use as a lamp base.

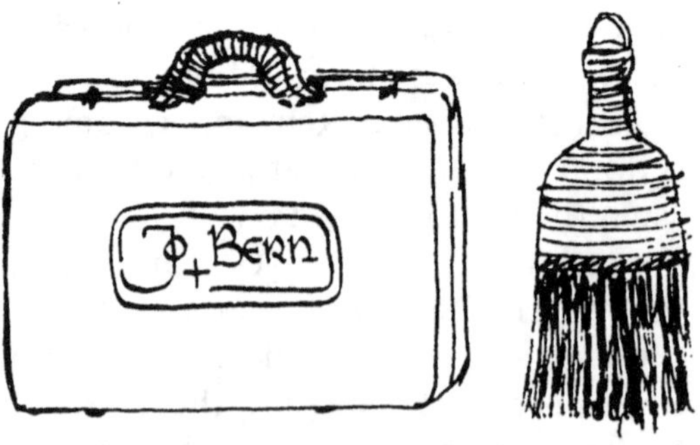

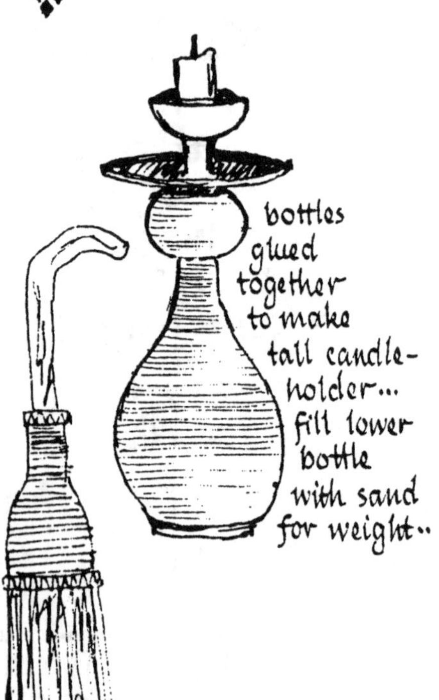

Tall candleholders can be made from stacked bottles and jars. Soak labels and glue off bottles. Stack with heaviest at bottom using various shapes for contrast and interest. Use silicone adhesive (for glass) to glue together where they touch. A good top is a sherbet glass attached right side up. Let set 24 hours to dry. Then paint with resin-based paint, which is thicker and needs only one coat (regular paint will also work). Decorate with twine, fabric, etc.

Wrap tin cans with twine to use as desk organizers.

CONTAINERS, ORGANIZERS, TRUNKS, BOXES, DRAWERS, BASKETS

This is a page of general ideas and techniques. By now you know the basics, have discovered how simple and logical is the process of pasting and covering, and that if you measured wrong, you managed to patch with confidence.

A small metal bucket can be covered with fabric inside, shellacked, then painted on the outside, with a fabric or paper cutout, wedding invitation, small postcard – something personal – as decoration. The handle can be wrapped with yarn or twine, bottom covered with fabric also. These are great for holding letters, pencils, kitchen spoons – whatever you wish.

Wastebaskets can be made from heavy round soap containers, large ice cream cartons, popcorn cans and other similar objects that may be available.

Boxes are wonderful to have as they help in organizing possessions such as jewelry, bobby pins, silverware, special collections, sewing, hair curlers, etc. Any kind of box will do. You know how to cover the sides of round and straight-sided boxes, so I'll discuss only the simple way of covering the inside bottom (same as tuna fish can cushion). Trace and cut a cardboard pattern slightly smaller than bottom of box. Then pull fabric over onto back of cardboard and fasten with glue. Remember, the paste will warp cardboard. Glue into bottom of box. When dry, this will take shellac as it is part of the solid box, and won't warp.

Cover a cardboard oatmeal box with fabric, insert at each side a velvet ribbon handle, strengthen bottom with cardboard and use as a knitting bag.

The tops of boxes are fun to decorate as they will hold three-dimensional objects, such as seashells, pearls, beads, coins, etc.

It's easy to make a top for a box using several thicknesses of cardboard. Glue thicknesses together and cover with fabric, which makes it quite strong. Hinges can be made with grosgrain ribbon, or folded fabric strip, applied with glue.

Box organizers for drawers can be constructed by using the following technique. Use heavy corrugated cardboard or several thicknesses of mat board. If strength is needed for bottom piece, use plywood or Masonite. Don't use paste for this; use only glue which dries fast. To make sides or dividers, cut the cardboard accurately with serrated knife or whatever tool you prefer. Use straight pins of hold sides together, push in with thimble. Cover corners with strips of sheeting or cotton bias tape, then cover the whole thing with fabric. Don't apply glue all over, just at strategic spots, such as corners.

I've made super purse-organizers this way. I first plan a size that fits in the purse, can be pulled out intact for changing. Mine has places for pencils, a comb, lipstick, two pairs of glasses, keys, notepads, scissors, nail file, date book, check book, handkerchief, card case, coin purse and billfold. I recommend this! People (especially men) are constantly surprised to see the rapidity with which I locate what I'm looking for.

When lining a drawer, use a strip of fabric that will go around all four sides. It should come just to the edges so it won't get in the way of pulling the drawer in and out. Then fit one piece of fabric in bottom of drawer. Shellac.

wastebasket made from cardboard container

tin bucket painted on outside lined with fabric......

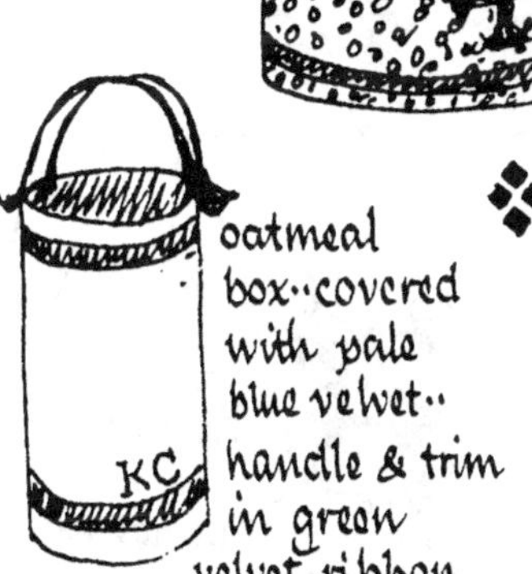

oatmeal box··covered with pale blue velvet·· handle & trim in green velvet ribbon

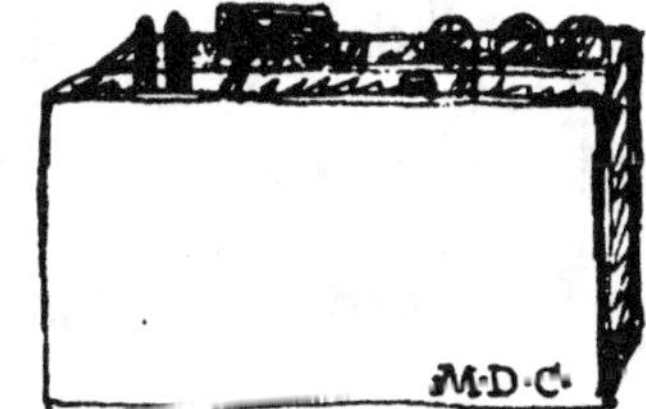

purse-organizer··strong & solid··2 long sections· lifts in & out of purse

Baskets are often lumpy and hard to line. Use paste on fabric and dot it here and there with glue. Between the two, you'll make it stick.

construct a deep cardboard frame to display a fan·· cover outside with velvet· line inside with fabric to match fan·· cut a piece of glass to fit·· glue in place, using upholstery braid··

I love to talk about trunks because I'm enthusiastic about the beautiful and practical things that can be done with them. In the first place, a trunk is something that can be used in nearly every room of the house for storage: in the front hall for boots, gloves, knit hats; in the living room for fireplace equipment, old newspapers, magazines, extra pillows; in the dining room for table cloths, overflow kitchen things; in bedrooms for blankets, linens, sweaters, sewing supplies, model airplanes; and on the back porch for tools and all that lands there. Trunks can be painted and fitted with a suitable lining, to go with any room. If flat-topped and strong, they can be used as benches, coffee tables or end tables. If "humpbacked," with the slats waxed and polished, they become a beautiful part of the room.

To line a trunk, follow instructions for lining a drawer. If trunk is large, you may want to use a separate piece of fabric for each side. The only problem that might arise is if there is rust inside. If so, shellac all inside areas after which you can paste with ease.

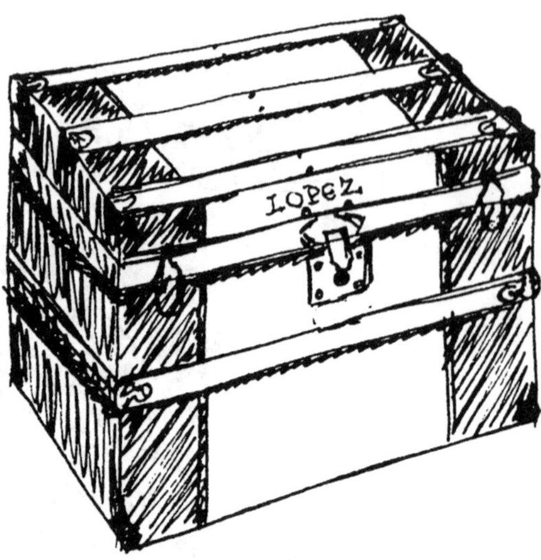

EGGS – STONES – MORE IDEAS

To make beautiful Christmas tree ornaments out of eggshells, first empty the shell: make holes in top and bottom of shell with hat pin. Then poke hat pin in hole and pierce yolk. Shake shell several times, blow through one hole, and the insides will come out easily. Now mark on shell with pencil where you want to cut, cover this line with several pieces of tissue paper and glue. Let dry. Mark again with pencil where you want to cut, then cut with manicure scissors, starting at hole in one end. The tissue paper gives such strength to the fragile shell that you can cut any shape you wish. To strengthen edge of shell, glue a piece of silk seam binding or fabric over edge. Then put any fabric you wish on both outside and inside. Trim with gold, beads, braid, or nylon net and put miniature figure or picture inside.

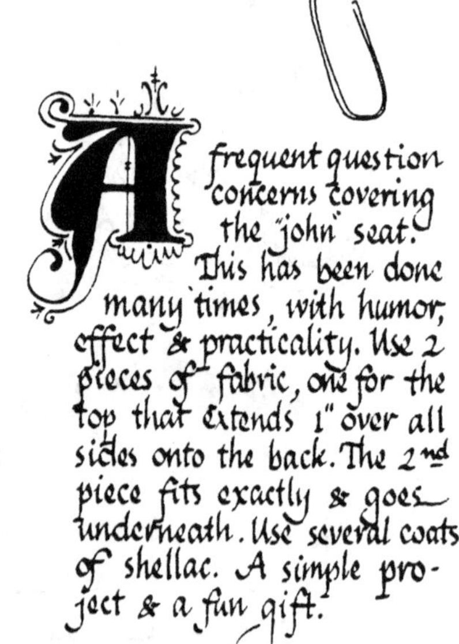

To make frame for this, cut a pattern of cardboard, fit carefully to edge of shell with nylon net or tissue paper. An effective way to cover eggs is with torn pieces of tissue paper in various colors. Use either glue with your fingers or brush on Liquitex Polymer medium (purchased at art supply store), which dries hard and strong. Then rub some treasure gold lightly over the ridged tissue paper for highlights. Make a little hanger of thread or gold cord.

A wooden box top or picture frame can be decorated with the delicate and beautiful eggshell mosaic or inlay. Rinse the broken eggshells, remove membrane from inside. Use Rit dye in hot water to color various shells. Lift out with tweezers, rinse in cool water and dry on paper towel. Apply glue to design on box or frame, and press eggshell into place until flat and dry. Use small pieces to fill in empty spaces in design. When dry, brush on shellac.

Do a tabletop with eggshell inlay in the natural tone that resembles finely-crushed ivory. It is easier to use large pieces of shell and when pressing onto surface, the weight will make small creases, hairlines and shatterings.

For another Christmas ornament, use half a nut shell, padded, in which to tuck a wee doll's head.

decorated eggshells

Egg-ideas: beautiful hung on a Christmas tree ∴ display a group of decorated eggs by hanging on a long velvet ribbon ∴ look for large goose-eggs to work with ∴ a good source of small pictures & icons to fit inside shells is the museum catalogue of reproductions ∴ display a special pendant or single earring (the mate of which is lost) in a velvet eggshell ∴

eggshell box ∴ standing on a small circlet of pearls ∴ outside covered with pale blue velvet ∴ inside with tissue paper ∴ hinge made by sewing over & over stitch in one place ∴

one-half eggshell, outside covered with mustard colored calico ∴ leather boot lacing glued around edge ∴ inside lined with gold foil, background for small madonna print ∴

a frame is made for eggshell from a thin piece of cardboard ∴ set in place with tissue-paper method ∴ cover all of shell & frame with colored tissue paper ∴ glue colored twine around 3 stones & edge of frame ∴ hanger is made of same twine ∴ rub all with Treasure Gold ∴

TISSUE-PAPER METHOD

of strengthening eggshells consists of tearing thin strips of tissue paper & applying several layers on top of one another ∴ Use white glue or Polymar Medium, which dries fast & gives remarkable strength to the fragile eggshell ∴ It can then be covered with fabric ∴ I also enjoy using various colors & shades of tissue paper on top of one another, which creates fascinating collages ∴ Rub Treasure Gold lightly over the wrinkled surface, for a delicate & ancient effect ∴

This technique can be used over cardboard or glass in many ways: on boxes, picture frames, bottles, windows, etc ∴

Let the kids make a patchwork eggshell — by pasting on small scraps & patches of calico ∴ Any shape will do — a fun project ∴

what a beautiful shape is the eggshell … what a beautiful shape is the eggshell …

As people have from earliest times, so have I enjoyed working with rocks and beautiful stones. I've collected white, round smooth stones at a certain beach in Milwaukee, and still have two boxes full that have traveled with me in various moves. And being a collector of proverbs, I letter a short saying on one side, using a regular pen and India ink. I paste calico on the back and cover the raw edges around edge of rock with leather shoelace or black middy braid applied with glue. If it is to be a hanging rock, I loop a piece of the shoelace or middy braid at the top for a small hook. Shellac entire rock several times. These are wonderful for gifts. For a special wedding gift, I letter names, date, etc., on front of rock, put leather over the back, then hang handmade Indian fetishes at the bottom. These stones make excellent paperweights.

hanging loop - goes around rock applied with glue-

SUPER–STICK PROCESS

It's also fun to make stone people and animals from various shaped stones, using the "super-stick process" as described below.

The "super-stick process" is used in gluing together two-dimensional objects. It involves equal amounts of cotton batting (purchased from the dime store) and glue, that's all. The remarkable holding quality results because of the combination of glue in the cotton fibers. I've repaired old santos, made little stone people, tightened wooden chair legs and have had fine luck with it for a long time.

I often mount small stones on box tops, plaques, bottles, etc., and set them with twine, just as a jeweler uses silver or gold.. I first put down a piece of cotton batting, drizzle some glue on it and push the stone down hard. Then I wrap the stone with jute twine and glue. When dry, I shellac the whole thing. Amazing!

For a special party, cover safety matchbooks with fabric. And for a special celebration or presentation of badges, make a medallion to wear on a ribbon. Use a tuna fish can lid or a circle of heavy cardboard. Cover with velveteen, jewels, and letter the proper title of the honoree for the center.

A good jewelry holder for the wall is made with a large gilded picture frame, centered with cushioned velveteen, pasted over foam rubber.

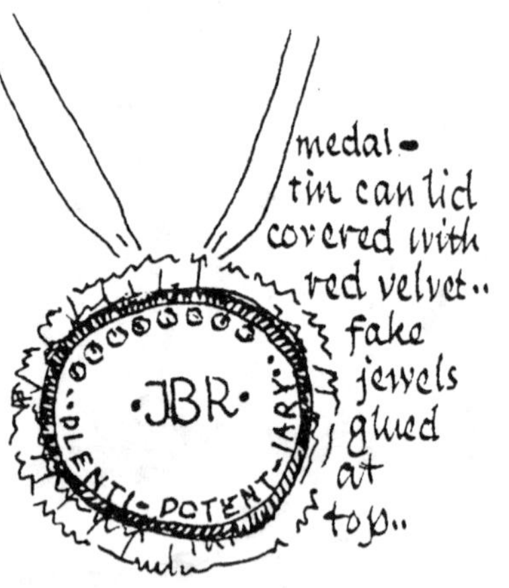

ROLL →
paper beads made from magazine ads cut in long triangular strips..
glue dot

A favorite of mine is paper beads. Find a good colored magazine ad, cut in long triangular strips, wrap around a small nail starting at the wide end. Roll up, secure at end with a dot of glue, slip off nail. Use nail polish or shellac to give a sheen to these beads. String on yarn, making a needle by rubbing glue on the end of the yarn and allowing to harden. A fine project for children.

do me a favor.. make some beads.. these are ordinary-looking things that must be experienced to be understood & enjoyed.. then teach someone else - share the fun..

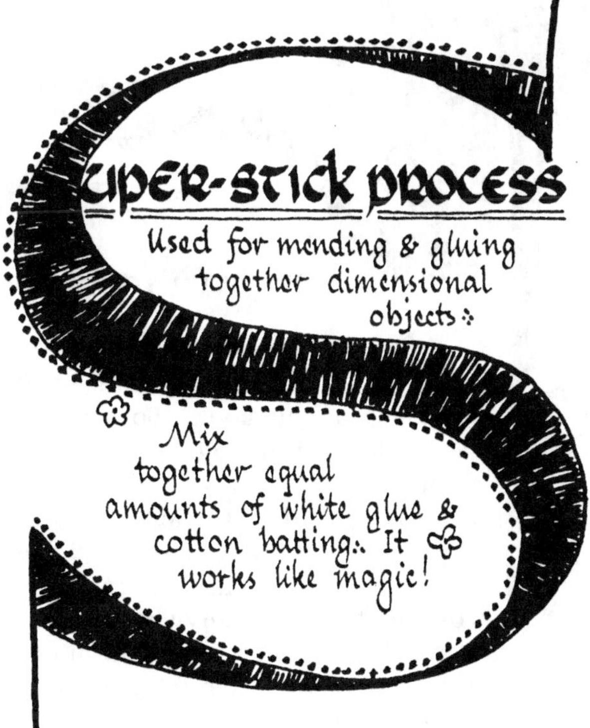

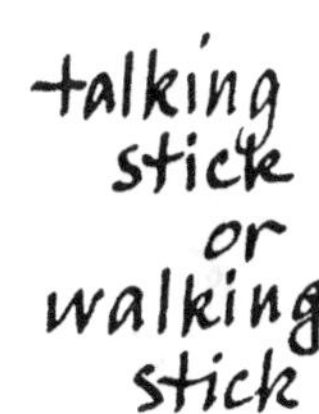

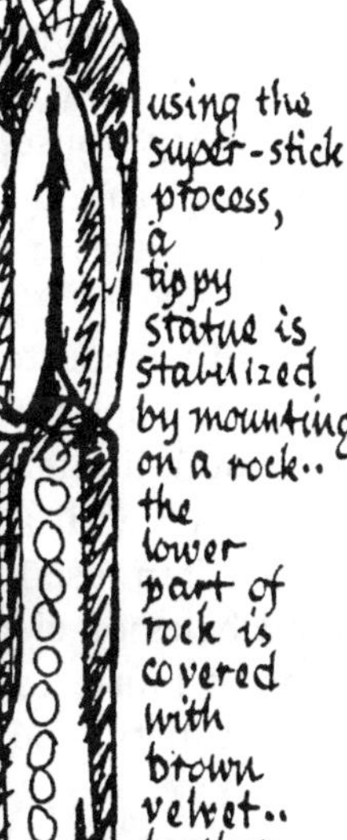

to mend or tighten a wobbly chair leg • turn chair upside down on table • remove or loosen the bad leg • squeeze Elmers into space • add tuft of cotton • then more glue • push leg firmly back into place • voila!

MORE IDEAS OF THINGS TO COVER:

- Flower pots
- Telephone book cover
- Seashells
- Wooden Bracelet
- Desk set
- Bed headboard
- Mirror frame
- Brick for doorstop
- Wooden clothes hangers
- Frame of kitchen clock
- Decoys
- Dictionary
- Sunglass frames
- Kleenex box
- Lap board
- Bulletin board
- File cabinet
- Metal trays
- Gourds from garden
- Window frames and sill

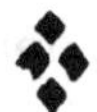

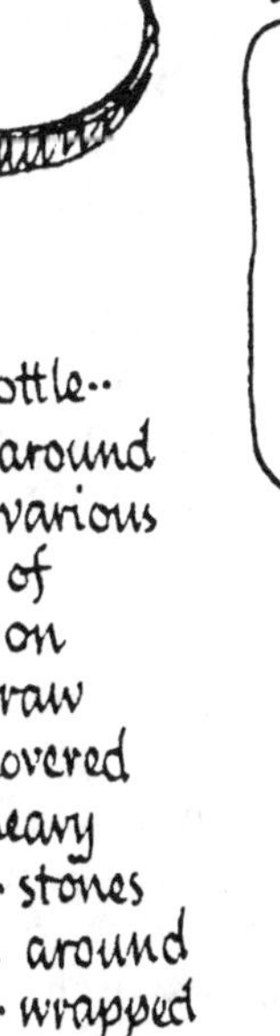

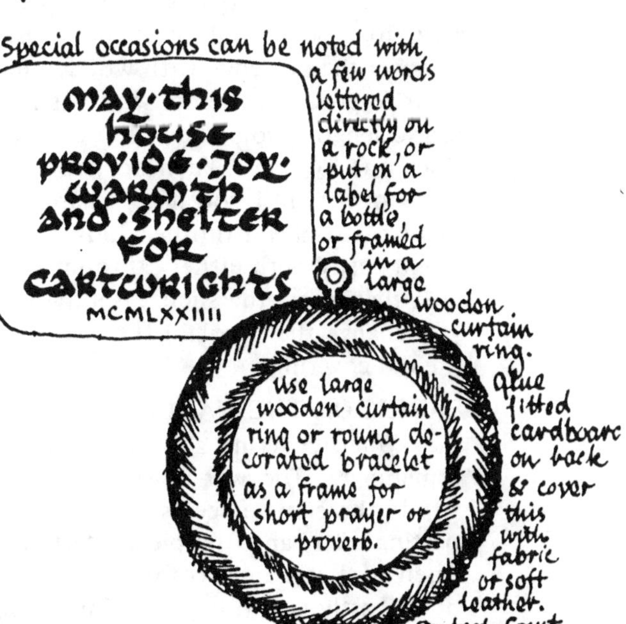

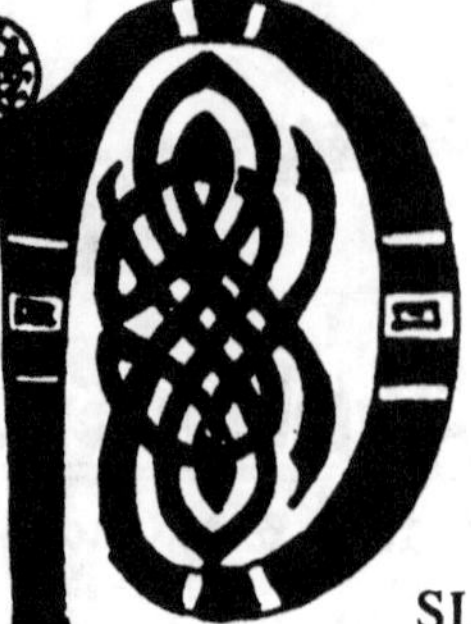

Paste Graduate Department

SLIP COVER YOUR FLOOR

So. . . . .Do you like pasting? Are you hooked? Here are some ideas of uncommon and fun things to do that you might not have considered at the beginning of this book. So have courage and get on with doing the things you really want to do in life; which applies not only to Pastecraft, but everything else. By now you've developed confidence in yourself, trained your eye to appropriate fabrics, etc., and now are relaxed enough to try something rather startling. We might as well consider slipcovering the floor. This is one of the most attractive, fun and inexpensive methods of floor covering to be seen anywhere under foot. I've done it – it was sensational! It was in a small entrance hall in our Kansas City house. I used red cotton plaid and repeated the fabric on picture mats. I found it practical and easy to maintain, and when it started to lose the protective finish, I simply put on several coats of shellac.

Slipcovering the floor is not a technically accurate description, but is close. To begin with, the only kind of floor to consider doing is one that is in bad condition. This technique works on wood, linoleum and clay tile.

There's nothing new in carpeting the floor with a cotton fabric since our grandmothers and great-grandmothers often used gingham or calico when times were hard. They spread several bales of clean wheat straw over the bare floor, sewed the necessary lengths of fabric together, spread it on the floor, and tacked it down. When it got dirty, they would take it up, wash it and put it down again.

Before starting, prepare surface so that it is smooth by filling cracks and holes as described in the Tabletop project. If working on a large area, you'll need to make gallons of paste, use a wide brush and dispense with a table and do all the work directly on the floor. Plan a strategy for proceeding from a corner to a doorway so you don't get yourself boxed in.

Use full lengths of fabric instead of short pieces. There are several ways to treat the fabric at the walls. Either fold the edges under 1/2 inch or cover the raw edge with wooden molding strips nailed down.

To proceed, select a sturdy, strong fabric, preferably a dark print. Your fabric lengths won't have to be sewed together: simply paste strips on the floor one by one. When dry, apply coats and coats of shellac, with the windows open, until you have a hard surface. If molding is being used, nail it in place to give a finished look and eliminate the fabric edge. This can be swept easily with either a broom or vacuum. If there is a particular traffic area that wears the shellac thin, give it an extra coat when necessary. When you change the decor in the room, simply paste your new fabric on top of the old covering.

IDEA! to get the look of small flagstones on an old floor (wood, linoleum, tile, cement): paste torn pieces of brown paper bags, with edges overlapping, all over floor.

While paper is still wet, brush paste on top surface to remove air bubbles. As it dries, the paper shrinks, giving a tight floor covering.

When dry, brush on 3 or 4 coats of shellac or bar varnish. This inexpensive floor-covering has a wonderful color & texture, with interesting free-form shapes. Delightful & fun to do!

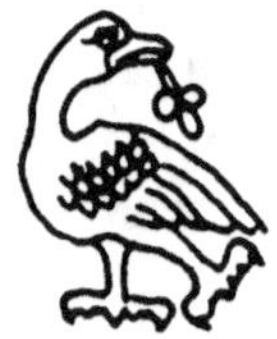

FABRIC ON THE WALLS

When covering a wall or ceiling with fabric there are several things to remember. The wet fabric is so heavy that you will need help in handling it. If the selvage seems to shrink when wet, it's best to remove it before pasting. To hang first piece, start at the top, getting it as straight as possible. Then trim top and bottom and rub well with your hands to get all bubbles out. Lastly, cut out pieces for the light switches but not before fabric is on wall.

COVER YOUR REFRIGERATOR

Planned or unplanned obsolescence aside, some of us tire of the whiteness of our refrigerators, even though they have good years of cooling our food and making ice cubes left. Perhaps you've longed to paint your refrigerator to match your kitchen decor, which would be a drastic and permanent step. But paint isn't the only way to effect a change; a better way is with fabric.

Measure sides, top and front of refrigerator, and figure how much fabric you'll need. If some is left over, use it to cover the bread box, frame several pictures, etc. The only difference in this and your first project, the wine bottle, is the fact that you may need two or more pairs of hands. It could be a family project that will probably be as much a memory-maker as any. Cut a hole for the door handle, and if you need to patch, this too is simple.

When covering the refrigerator door, bring the fabric to the outside edge. It should not go inside. If the brand name is on the door, it is easier to cover it. It will be lumpy but this can't be helped.

When dry, shellac for protection against future scrubbing. Should you ever want to remove the fabric, you can with difficulty, as it will be stuck very hard. You'll also find grains of shellac, which penetrated the fabric onto the porcelain enamel surface. Please give this consideration before starting the pasting job.

A second solution to covering the refrigerator is to use a plastic paper (Con-tact), to be found in dime stores and other places. This can be removed when necessary, leaving no traces of your camouflage. Our brick refrigerator in Milwaukee caused as much comment as anything in the house, as it also did when it was pine-panelled.

MEMO:

HAVE·YOU·THANKED·YOUR·TEACHERS? Teachers are to be found in schools, as well as almost everyplace else. Teachers are trained in schools. Also some of the best teachers have learned valuable lessons & basic philosophies from everyday experiences in living. Good teachers like to share what they know.

We must consciously realize which "teachers" have influenced our lives — & then tell them about it! Often the application of things learned occurs long after a class is finished, so the teacher has no idea for whom he has opened a door.

A teacher once told me that about one former student a year gets in touch with him to tell him of his personal or intellectual growth & to express some degree of gratitude.

Teachers are human beings & so enjoy personal, warm responses to their efforts.

HAT AND COAT RACK

put clothes-hooks on long fabric-covered board by front or back door···for guests' and occupants' hats, umbrellas, coats, ponchos, catchers' mitts, whatever···

POOR MAN'S BOOKCASE

This is a standby of college professors, writers, *New Yorker* editors, newly-marrieds, poor people who like to read, and magazine collectors. It's a great space-filler, adds style and warmth to a room, and of course has multitudinous uses other than for books.

Locate second grade lumber and old bricks. Paste fabric on top and sides of boards, then shellac. Build the bookcase by arranging bricks so that they support the shelf in three places. Then lay on the first board, and build three more stacks of bricks. Lay on the next board. You can stop here or go higher. The top can be used either as a seat or a shelf, depending on the height. For a special effect, the bricks can be painted.

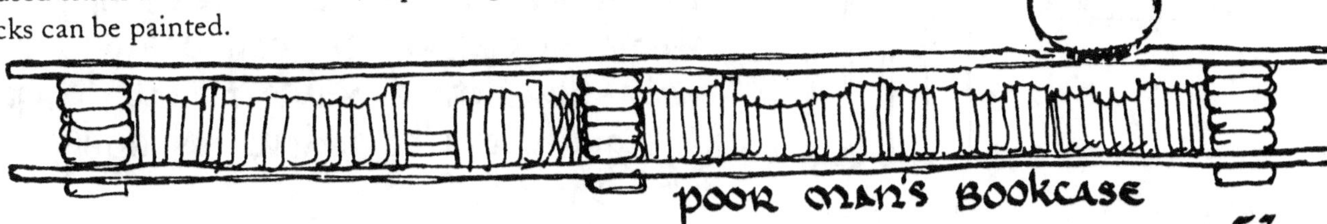

To make 6'3" tall

GREEK COLUMNS

which was done by the Junior Art Museum of the Des Moines Art Center in 1965 ~ in constructing a temple replica as part of an Ancient Greek Art exhibit.

They first built skeleton frames of thin strips of wood ~ then used tubs of paste & yards of unbleached muslin to cover the frames, shaping the fabric in between the slats to form a concave curve. The fabric was extremely heavy, needing about 4 people to handle it. They improvised a way of pressing fabric to the strips ~ by using a block-printing rubber roller.

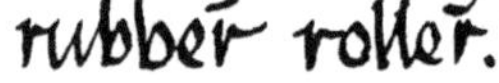

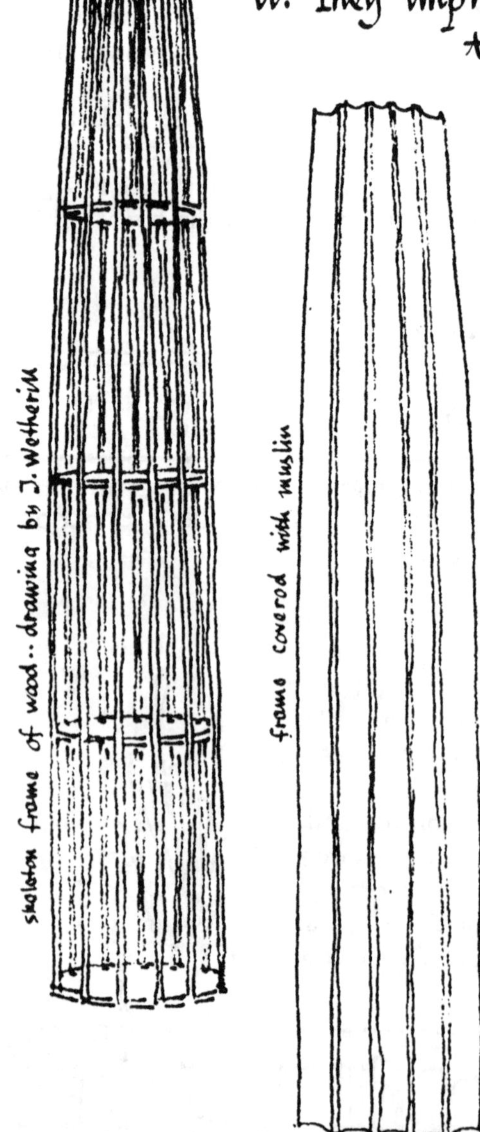

skeleton frame of wood .. drawing by J. Wetherill

frame covered with muslin

When dry, the top & bottom were trimmed ~ & then the entire surface was coated with white latex paint. The 8 columns proved to be sturdy & durable ~ as they withstood 8 months of childrens' testing & admiration. They never needed repair! A remarkable solution, demonstrating the advantage of fabric over papier mâché.

This technique of using muslin over a frame & then painting it ~ can be applied to LARGE STAGE PROPS or OTHER OUTSIZE PROJECTS. If a free form is to be used, the skeleton frame can be made with wire instead of wood. SCULPTURE can be done with this method ~ additional strength & rigidity can be achieved by applying first shellac & then paint.

TO INSULATE CEMENT BLOCK WALLS & FLOORS

This technique works wonders with cement block walls and floors of homes in housing projects. Plug and fill all cracks with torn newspaper strips dipped in paste. Paste several layers of newspaper over surface to be covered, then cover with fabric or paint.

SOME INSIDE–OUTSIDE IDEAS

Several pasters have lined the insides of their VW buses or mobil homes with fabric. Some have covered the rural mailbox by the road or covered glass bathroom windows. A Des Moines paster turned an old bathroom into a charming spot that everyone walks upstairs to see. Everything was in white tile so she used yards and yards of red calico in her renovation – for the dado strip of wood around the walls, on the ceiling underneath the footed bathtub, and even on the "john" seat.

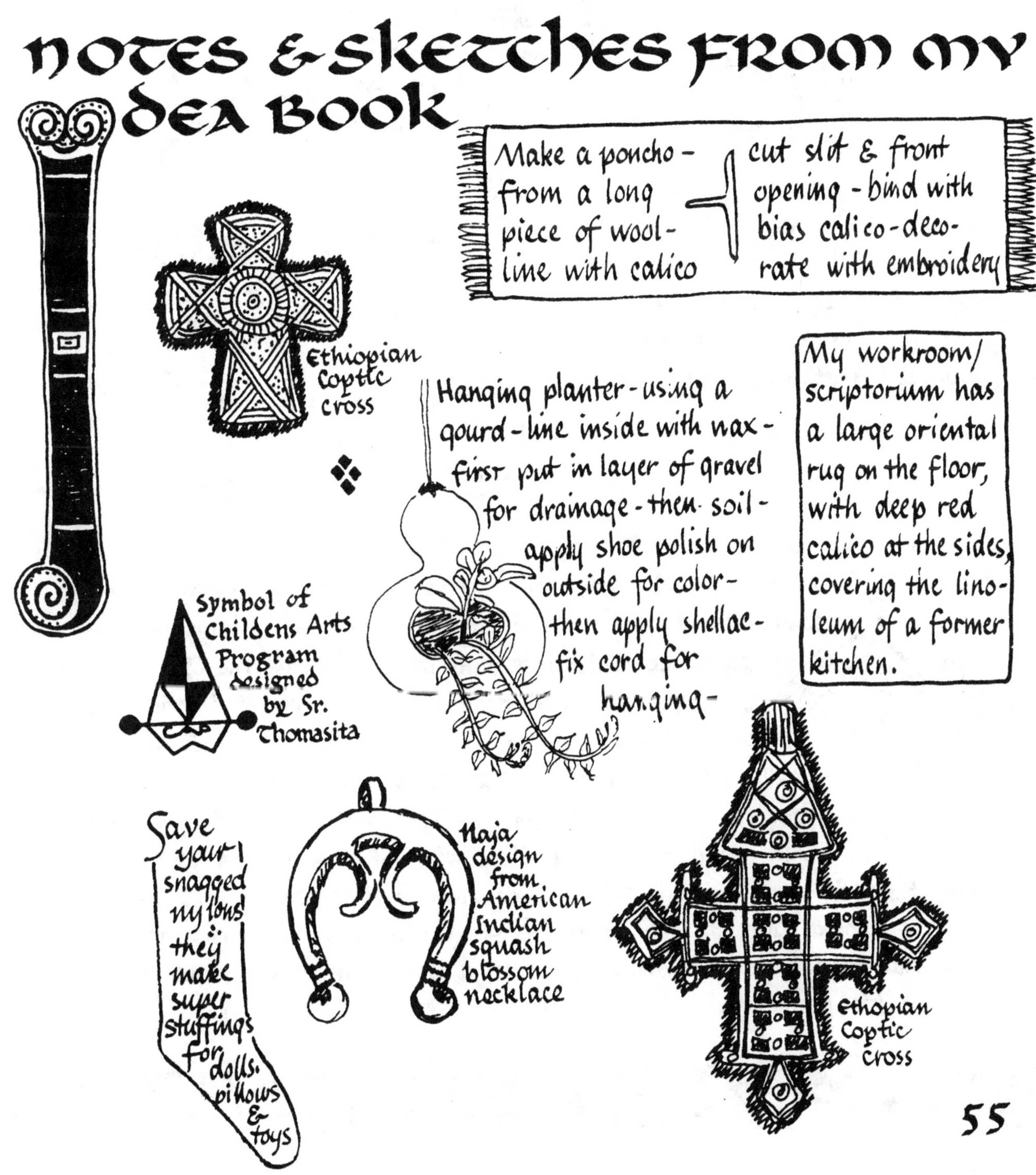

Design a personal craft mark, using 2 or 3 initials. Make dozens of sketches & arrangements until you have a good one. Use for signing your work, for embroidery, stationery, etc.

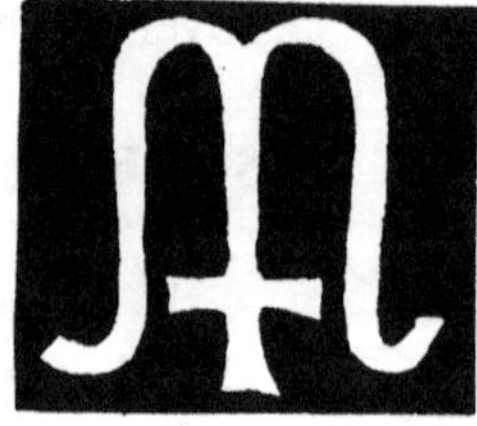

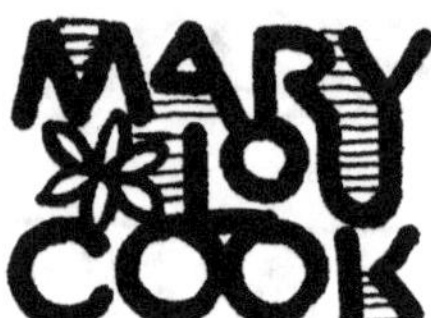

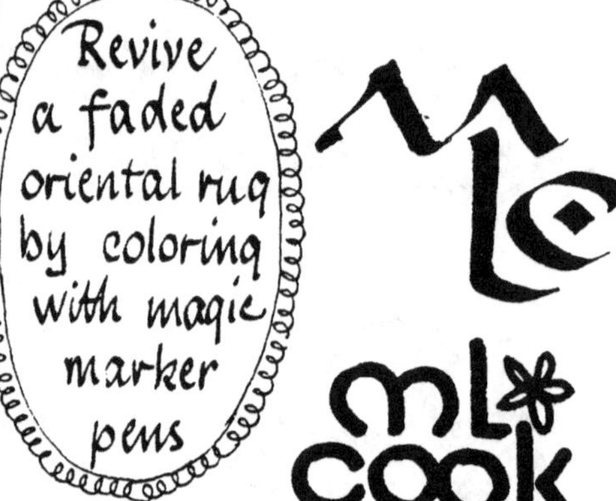

Revive a faded oriental rug by coloring with magic marker pens

Make a soft book of unbleached muslin - cut the edges w/ pinking shears - sew together in center - do writing w/ thin magic marker pen - decorate w/ buttons. embroidery. etc.

Cover pillows with remants of oriental rugs - back with velveteen - rich and beautiful!

OJO·DE·DIOS

Spanish for eye of God, a folk art found in many cultures, some going back to ancient civilizations, steeped in religious signifinence. The Huichol Indians of Mexico use the OJO today, believing the symbol wards off evil spirits & brings protection & blessings upon the user. TO WEAVE an OJO, you'll need several colors & 2 sticks. Hold sticks in left hand in form of cross, bind together at center & wrap tightly 4 times with yarn, using right hand. Then wrap over & around each stick one time & move to next stick, going counter-clockwise. Always wrap over & around each stick one time. To start new color, cut first yarn & tie ends together. My favorite folk art ~ a good learning experience for the "veriest beginner."

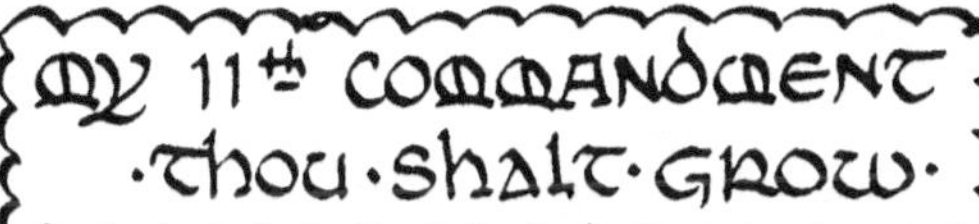

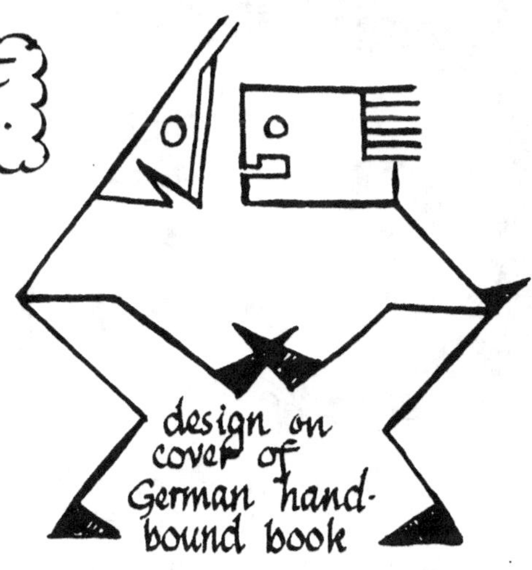
design on cover of German hand-bound book

MEMO: Look for the simple way to live with style & creativity— Enter competitions, push yourself to experiment & learn & produce— Remember the key to understanding is respect— Locate Recreation Labs in your area, a re-freshing week with great people—

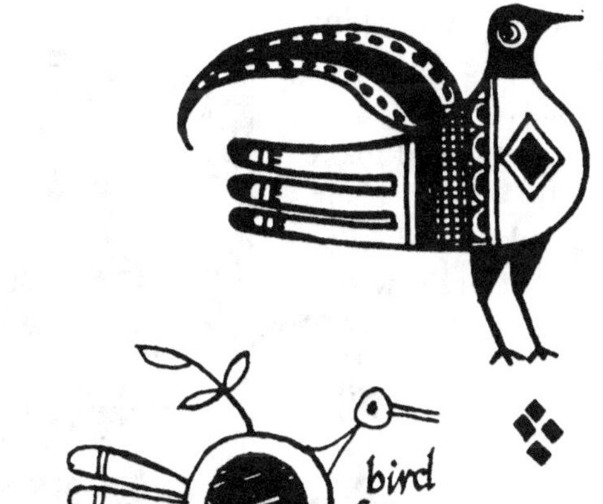
bird from American Indian pottery

Use unbleached muslin to make banners, such as pictured on back cover. Letter with felt-tipped pen, then decorate by sewing on braids, ribbon & calico. Put calico on back.

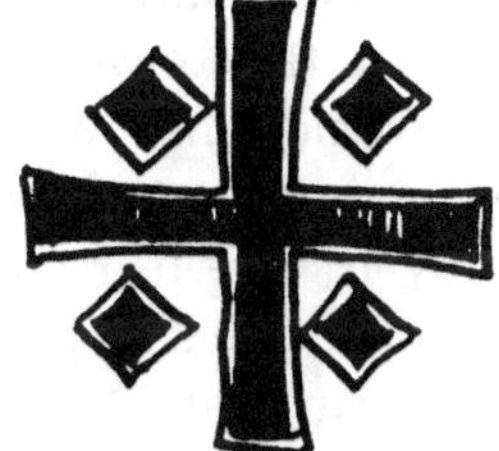

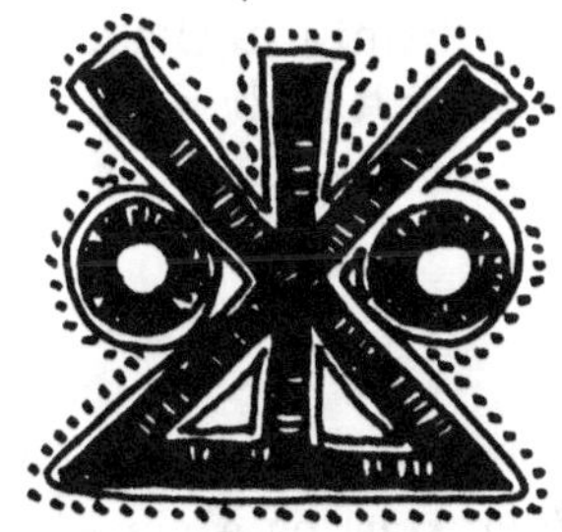

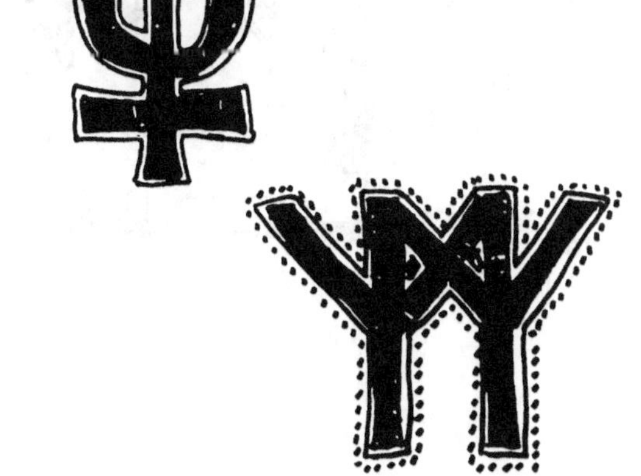

Clay-Bake (to make bread-dough figures) mix 4 c. flour, 1 c. salt, 1½ c. water — knead until pliable-work on waxed paper bake 1 hour in 300° oven - prick when it puffs up - shellac for glisten & sheen—

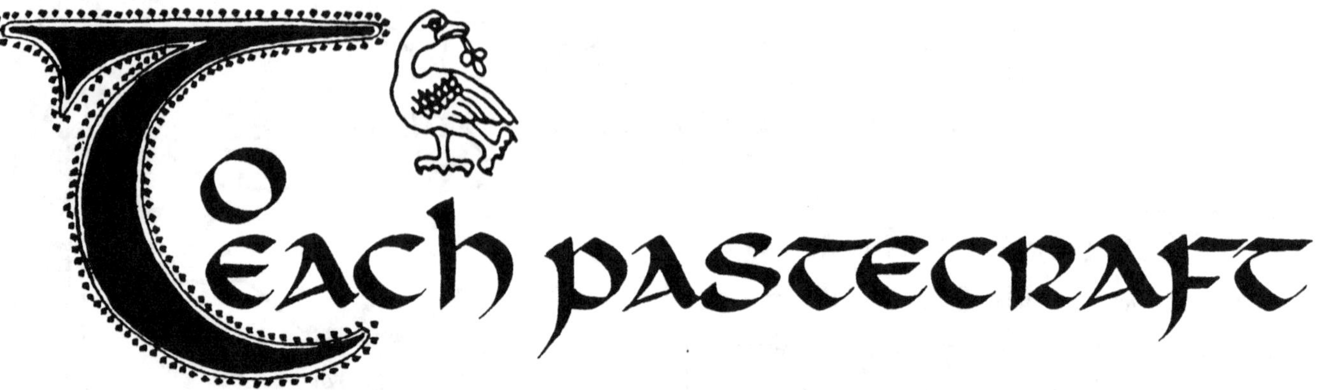

Teaching is a matter of sharing something about which one is enthusiastic and knowledgeable. Teaching is communicating, working with a group for which one has respect, leading and then encouraging members of the group in turn to teach and share. Teaching is being sensitive to response – and listening, listening, listening. Teaching is believing in people and bringing out the best in them.

Your friends may want you to teach them how to paste, or the adult education program may invite you to give a class. If so, and if you think you'd enjoy it, give it a try. But don't attempt to teach anyone until you have had experience as a paster and have confidence in yourself.

In preparing for a class, I organize everything ahead of time and make sure the equipment is in good order. Each participant should have a chair, enough table space for a spread-out newspaper, a wastebasket and good light. It is helpful to have one extra table to use as an exhibit area, with a cloth to cover it and an exhibit of Pastecraft "pieces" for ideas.

When starting a class or workshop, which should start and end on time, I begin by talking about me, about who I am, what things I value, a bit of my philosophy. (One of my inspirational teachers was Dr. Henry Nelson Wieman, the great theologian of Grinnell, Iowa.) Then I ask class members in turn to do the same, and in ten minutes we have a group that is in touch with one another, where every person has had a chance to be heard and is now ready for a special learning experience. The sharing that happens in a group is warm and wonderful and the new ideas that go back and forth are most exciting.

Instruction should be given one step at a time with the assumption that everyone is a beginner. Check carefully to see that each person comprehends before moving on. Ask for questions at any time. This should be an informal and fun experience.

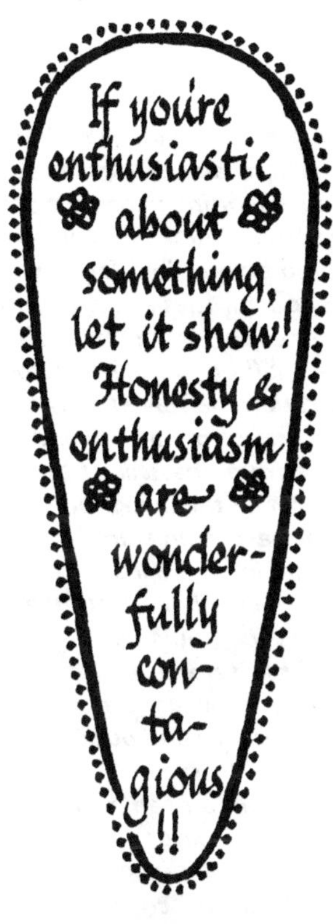

After everyone is into pasting, I go around the room quietly, looking thoughtfully and carefully at each person's work. My purpose is to find something good in each piece or something in the person's attitude that is positive. I make it a point to mention softly to this person what I have observed. I make only one comment, which is always honest, as I can find

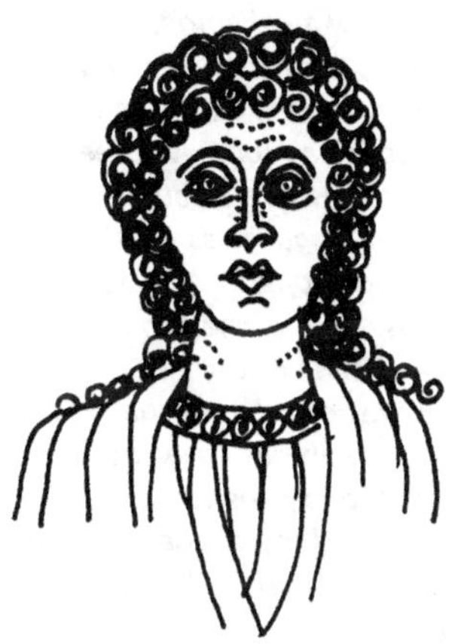

something good in every person and his work. (Conversely, if I were looking for mistakes, I could also find them, but that isn't my idea of encouraging people toward learning.)

I like to plan and work toward an exhibit at the end of the class, which gives incentive to make an extra effort to finish a project. The total effect is exciting, another step in the growth of a person's skills.

I strongly suggest that all craftsmen sign their work with name and date. This signifies pride in the job he's done and that he's done his best. I also suggest that he accept all compliments on his work with two words, "Thank you," never an apology or explanation of his shortcomings and inadequacies. We must learn to respect ourselves and our work.

I hope you'll consider teaching. If you think you've had fun *learning* Pastecraft, wait until you get into *sharing* it with a bunch of kids or your neighbors. This is one of the best prescriptions and solutions I know for the human problems around us.

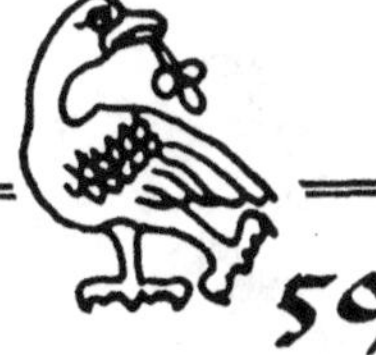

Quotes from Pasters

Pastecraft starts a whole new way of thinking. Expensive decorating ideas become an inexpensive reality. The techniques taught can be applied to modern shapes and textures as well as antique and provincial. . . . I'm thrilled with this new awakening. . . . I have some questions about applying needlepoint to baskets and book covers that need your professional answer. . . . Thank you for removing artificial limits. . . . Your class is one of the most exhilarating experiences I've ever had. I feel your course should be required for all young homemakers. How could anyone ever feel "trapped" again with such creative opportunities at our fingertips? . . . . The Vista Volunteers were discussing the value of Mrs. Cook's classes for all people, that these crafts are as much a universal language as music. . . . Found making paper beads with a small boy in our disturbed children nursery a good project. Although he has very short periods of concentration, he stayed busy and happy for 45 minutes. . . . I learned to have pride in my work, as it's done to the best of my ability and when being praised, I'll say "thank you". . . . operating on a slim but secure budget, I've found pastecraft to be my answer to home decoration. Lamp shades have taken on character, and are an asset to the living room. An old office desk and file cabinet have found a place in our TV room. Pictures that have been stored away because framing was too expensive have brightened the dining room wall. Gift-making has become practical, inexpensive and fun. And my husband has a pot of "Mary Lou paste" for his work bench. . . . Enthusiastic reaction to your class with our Salvation Army people. May God's richest blessings be yours. . . . You certainly have taken the town over, I see the results everywhere. . . . Our last child has just left home and this new craft is proving to be most satisfying at a time when I really need it. . . . It can't help but make me a more joyous person, which benefits both my family and friends. . . . Your wonderful exuberance and outlook on life, your sharing of yourself, have truly been one of my most treasured experiences. . . . I learned of pastecraft from my grandmother, who took your class. I won a blue ribbon at the county fair and am working on a fourth demonstration of pastecraft. . . . Thanks for the inspiration to attempt creating, however crude the result may be. There is a certain joy in being original. . . . It seems the Junior League has the two-party system now—the pasters and the non-pasters. . . . A group of us women who work at the Pella Rolscreen factory are interested. . . . I'm Cubmaster of Local Pack 101, BSA, and we are always interested in low-cost craft ideas. . . . Such fun, everyone should be made to do it!!! So much for so little. It's a bit of a disease with me now. I can't stop pasting. . . . The glow really didn't come until you showed your slides. They are beautiful, hit me the same way as "My Fair Lady". . . . Thank you for two weeks of enlightenment. . . . I've learned many new ways of doing things the easy way. Now one idea seems to hatch another. It's exciting and you made it all possible. . . . Pastecraft is the greatest! The tools are easily assembled, the working space so versatile that I can work in any room in the house without muss or fuss, even on a TV tray. . . . It is amazing when I think of all the places and things I can do over with pastecraft. . . . Few crafts have such limitless possibilities. . . . A blending of old ideas and new techniques. . . . I have greatly enjoyed these classes for many reasons, but the most important is that I find myself being creative in every other area. . . . We love the new effect of an old eye-sore, our hi-fi redone in fabric. . . . A delight, one project gives birth to two more . . . . The crafts shown on your TV show were next to unbelievable. . . . I covered doors, inset panels of kitchen cabinets, window shades, and the underneath of the bathtub, which is filled with house plants, all for $11.25. . . . I never imagined there could be so many interesting things to do, makes me want to quit my job and just paste. . . . Have never been so happy to be a woman. . . . Fantastic is the only word to describe your paste recipe! I've used it with exceptionally dark, expensive, and heavy fabrics in my professional decorating commissions. The results are amazing because even though the material was completely wet when placed on the wall, it dried to its original color. . . . Has my mind swimming with ideas. How refreshing to be given new

thoughts, to learn new areas of creativity. . . . I've gained courage to try. . . . Be assured that Mary Lou's spiritual message is getting across. . . . My only lament is that ideas for using this come far faster than I can carry them out. . . . I hope you can keep this craft to the high artistic level that you personally espouse and teach. . . . The whole family is having fun framing their collections. . . . Pastecraft can be used in every home, a craft one should be acquainted with like knitting or sewing. . . . There are some old hymnals in church that might be improved through the use of cloth and this special paste. . . . The people in our psychiatric department are still buzzing with enthusiasm about the refreshing and recreative time they had with you. . . . I saw your students' exhibit and thought it was beautiful; have you ever thought about coming to St. Louis?. . . . In the 8 years I've had the TV program, few if any have been received more enthusiastically. . . . As most of us are house-bound with young children, you gave us many ideas to develop our creativity and our children's. . . . It may be as artistic or as practical as one may choose, the true enjoyment grows with its use. . . . The potential value of such knowledge is unlimited. How rewarding to create something attractive from an item that you would normally discard. . . . With paste and fabric nearly anything can be salvaged, redeemed, transformed, created. . . . Jim and I made a playhouse for the girls' Christmas surprise, using a huge TV shipping carton. It has a door, windows, a pointed roof, red velvet chimney, flowers around the base, and is named "The Three Dears". . . . I'm planning to make a corner for myself in the basement, getting my pastecraft equipment all in one place, and using the ping-pong table to work on. . . . A skill I'll use all my life. . . . Every time I've walked in your door my eyes light up and my heart beats faster in anticipation of what I'll learn and better, what I'll hear. . . . In the past, I've never attempted any type of project such as you taught. Now I have confidence I shall be able to create. . . . . Thank you for passing on some of your knowledge, ideas, and your wonderful enthusiasm. You've given many people a new challenge to find beauty in the common things around them. . . . I don't know how the recipient of the gift may feel, but there is an awful lot of myself in the object, more than if I bought a gift in a store. Besides the pleasure, pastecraft provides the opportunity to forget the everyday world and be refreshed in mind and spirit. . . . My friends and neighbors are so enthusiastic about pastecraft that I may end up teaching them how to do it. . . . But now we paste proficiently and proudly sign our names. . . . I've been hearing wonderful reports about your classes in Kansas City. . . . The students of the New Mexico State School for the Deaf were impressed with this unique experience. . . . Recently on a homes tour a woman was heard commenting on some of the things I'd pasted in the kitchen: "You can certainly tell these people have traveled a lot, just look at all the things from Europe.". . . . The pregnant teenagers group showed obvious enthusiasm. . . . Your own enthusiasm is contagious. . . . You gave us so much more than pastecraft. . . . An inspiring teacher. Her students leave her classes feeling ten feet tall. Her warm praise unfolds the creativity that most of us never knew we had. . . . A virtuoso in paste. . . . Serendipity is one of MLC's gifts, finding valuable and agreeable things not sought for. . . . MLC has the kind of creative imagination and artistic ability which one rarely encounters in today's world. Her enthusiasm encourages even the most timid would-be craftsman or artist to try his hand. . . . Her work is a refreshing change from the ordinary things offered currently as "handiwork" or "hobbies." She does not jealously guard her secrets but shares them with all who might be interested. . . . Her qualities of greatness lie primarily in the fact that she has always wanted to bring out the best in and for people and to enhance all material things around her. . . . A born teacher. . . . I thought of pastecraft in Haiti for the native people, some handicapped, some not; it would be exactly right. . . . A successful way to communicate with the families in our Peace Corps village. . . .

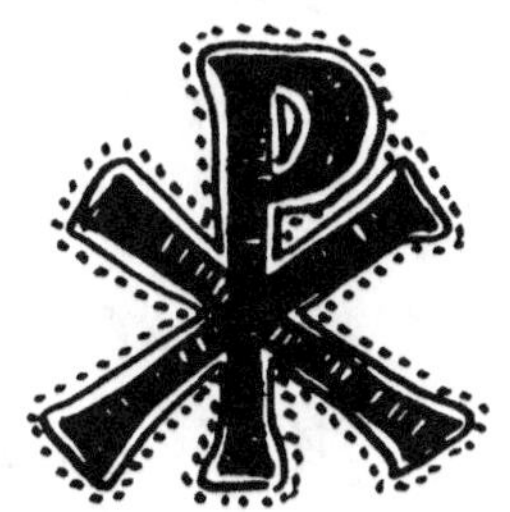

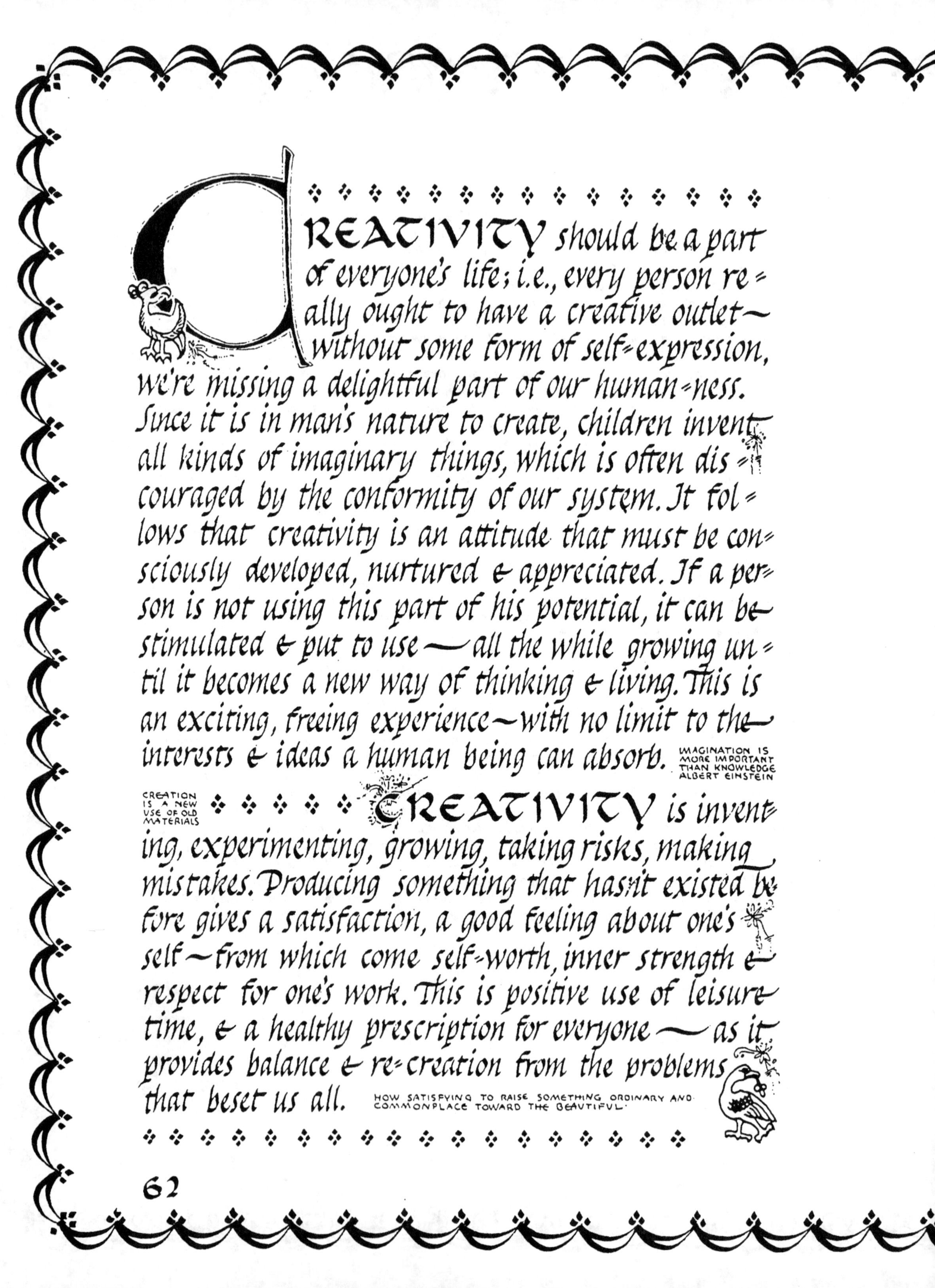

CREATIVITY should be a part of everyone's life; i.e., every person really ought to have a creative outlet—without some form of self-expression, we're missing a delightful part of our human-ness. Since it is in man's nature to create, children invent all kinds of imaginary things, which is often discouraged by the conformity of our system. It follows that creativity is an attitude that must be consciously developed, nurtured & appreciated. If a person is not using this part of his potential, it can be stimulated & put to use — all the while growing until it becomes a new way of thinking & living. This is an exciting, freeing experience—with no limit to the interests & ideas a human being can absorb.

IMAGINATION IS MORE IMPORTANT THAN KNOWLEDGE ALBERT EINSTEIN

CREATION IS A NEW USE OF OLD MATERIALS

CREATIVITY is inventing, experimenting, growing, taking risks, making mistakes. Producing something that hasn't existed before gives a satisfaction, a good feeling about one's self—from which come self-worth, inner strength & respect for one's work. This is positive use of leisure time, & a healthy prescription for everyone — as it provides balance & re-creation from the problems that beset us all.

HOW SATISFYING TO RAISE SOMETHING ORDINARY AND COMMONPLACE TOWARD THE BEAUTIFUL.

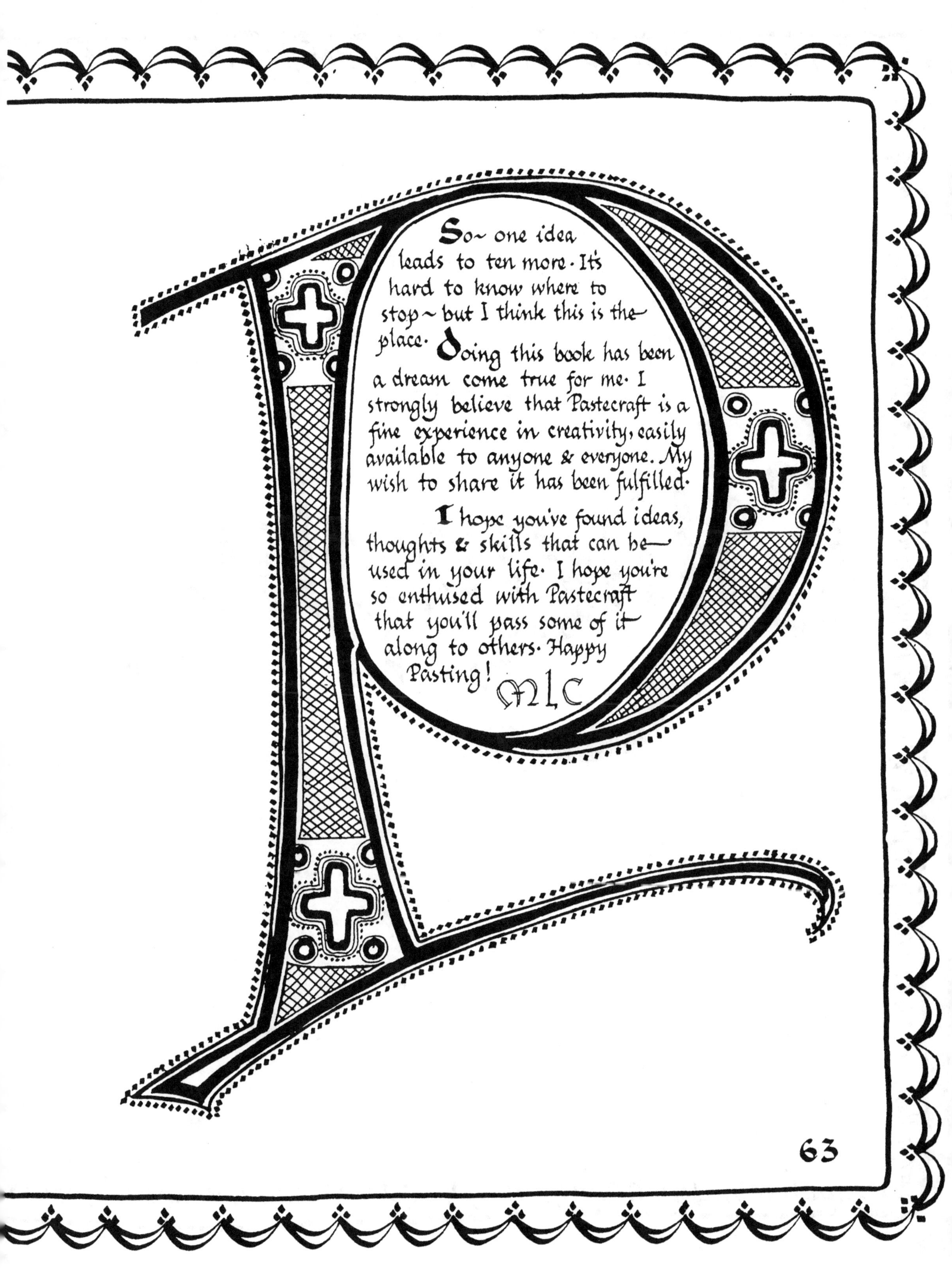
So~ one idea
leads to ten more. It's
hard to know where to
stop ~ but I think this is the
place. Doing this book has been
a dream come true for me. I
strongly believe that Pastecraft is a
fine experience in creativity, easily
available to anyone & everyone. My
wish to share it has been fulfilled.
I hope you've found ideas,
thoughts & skills that can be
used in your life. I hope you're
so enthused with Pastecraft
that you'll pass some of it
along to others. Happy
Pasting!
MLC

wxyzabcdefghijklmnopqrstuvwxyzabcdefghijklmnopqrstuvwx

Calligraphy

Calligraphy

This section on Calligraphy is a joyful addition to Pastecraft. Now two passions of my life are under one cover. These years as a scribe have been deeply satisfying, as the pleasures of hand lettering are endless. To me it is the human touch of spirit, beauty & heart that speaks to the soul. Called 'every man's art,' calligraphy is practical & efficient for daily use, & beautiful for writing poetry & certificates.

Included in this section are ideas & designs for quotes, certificates, thank yous, free notes, invitations, etc; as well as basic hand writing instructions. You are welcome to copy & use as you wish. Lastly, you may want to find a calligrapher in your area who will do beautiful invitations & other personal work.

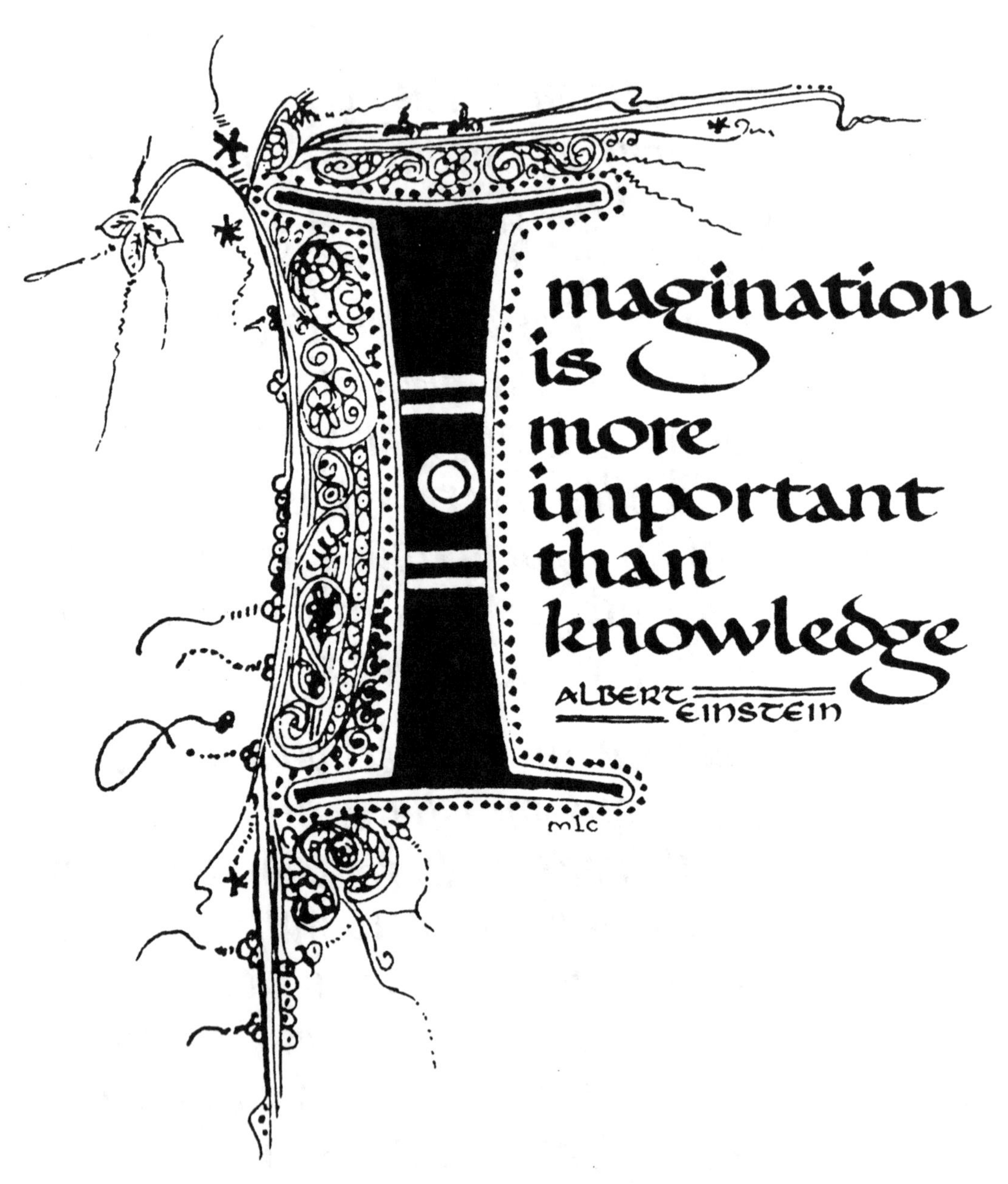

This is a 'Broadside', a piece written on one side only, to be hung.

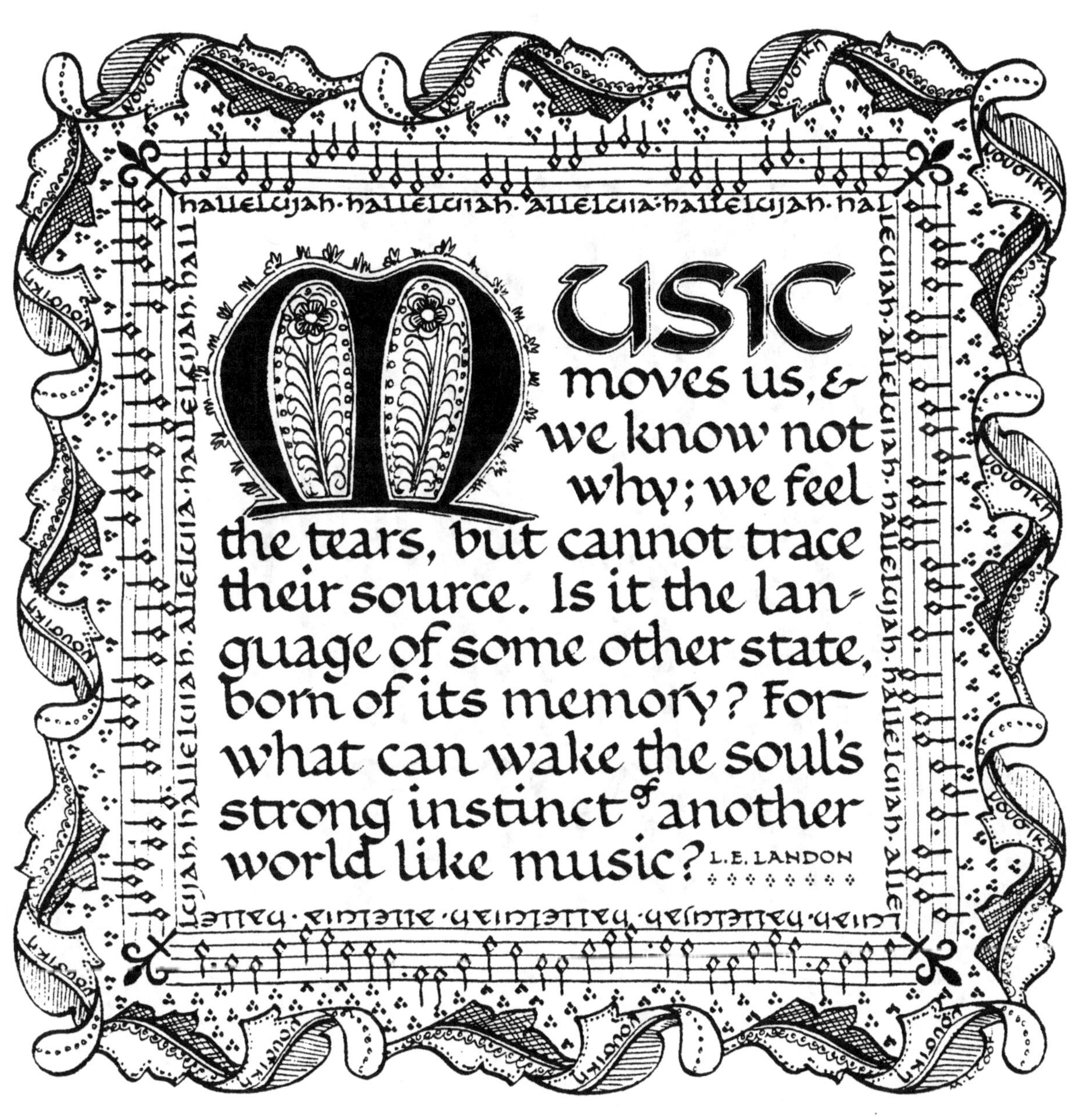

All of these pieces can be reduced or enlarged for reproduction.

listening fingers know the heart's intent

·mlc·

Written for acupuncturists & body workers.

WE
MUST·TURN
TO·OURSELVES
AS·A·CREATIVE·PIECE
OF·WORK — NOT
ONLY·IN·THE·ARTS,
BUT·IN·THE
CREATION·OF
OUR·LIVES

ANAÏS NIN

SCRIPSIT
MARY LOU
COOK
MCMLXXXXI

Anaïs Nin is a brilliant diarist & my second cousin.

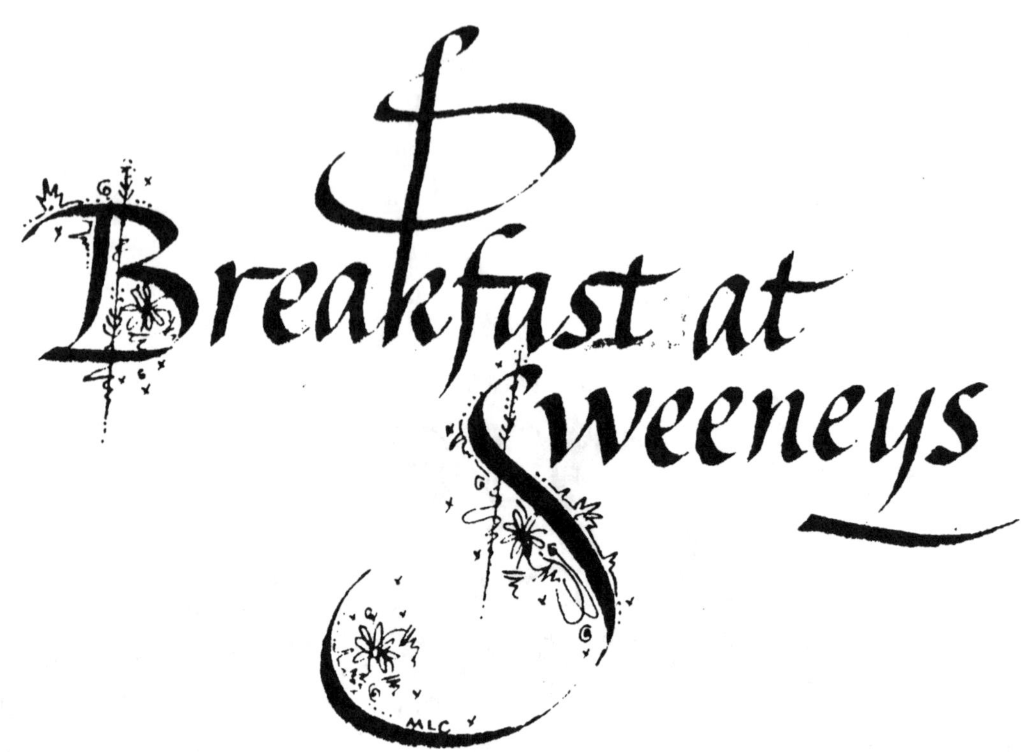

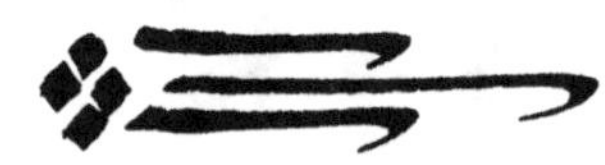

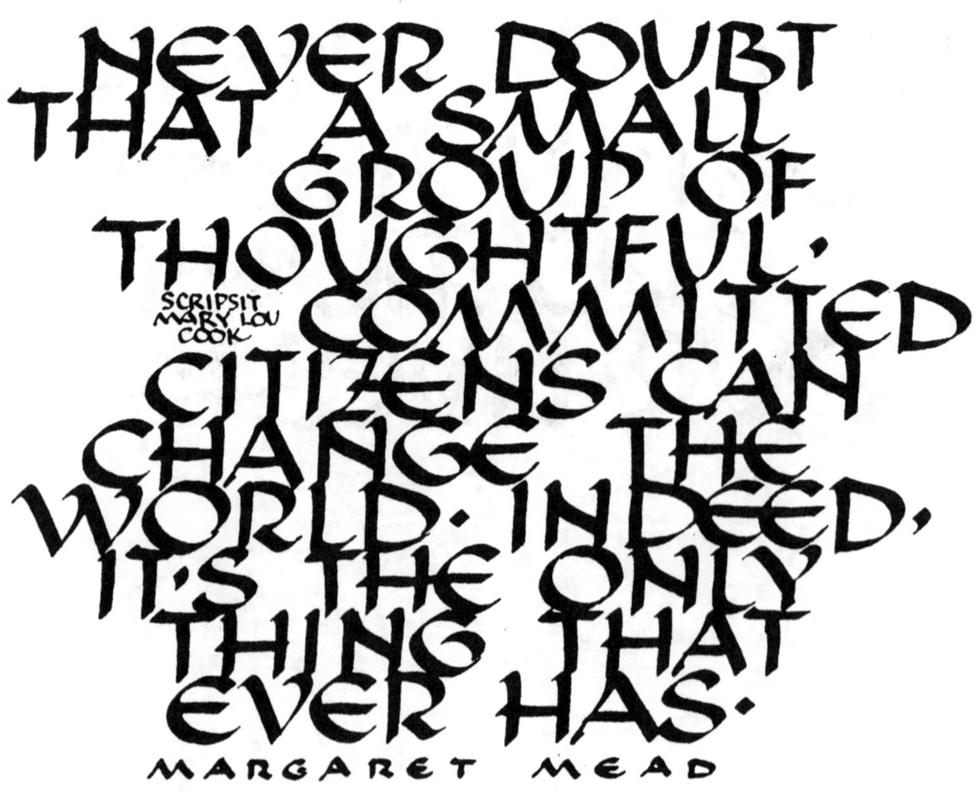

The Mead quote is especially appropriate for activists.

this instant is the only time there is

THE PAST IS OVER IT CAN TOUCH ME NOT

FROM A COURSE IN MIRACLES

M.L.C.

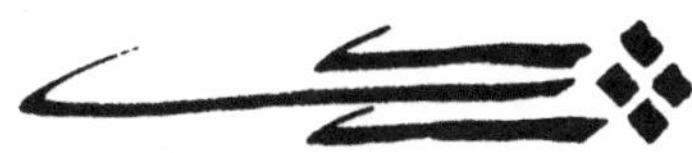

forgiveness is the key to happiness

M.L.COOK

MY THOUGHTS ARE IMAGES I HAVE MADE. I CAN ELECT TO CHANGE ALL THOUGTS THAT HURT. FROM A COURSE IN MIRACLES

Some spiritual quotes.

HARRY; CHRISTMAS 1976 ~ WITH LOVE, BETTY

You cannot bring about prosperity by discouraging thrift. You cannot help the wage-earner by pulling down the wage-payer. You cannot further the Brotherhood of Man by encouraging class hatred. You cannot help the poor by destroying the rich. You cannot keep out of trouble by spending more than you earn. You cannot build character and courage by taking away a man's initiative. You cannot help men permanently by doing for them what they could and should do for themselves.

MLC

ABRAHAM LINCOLN

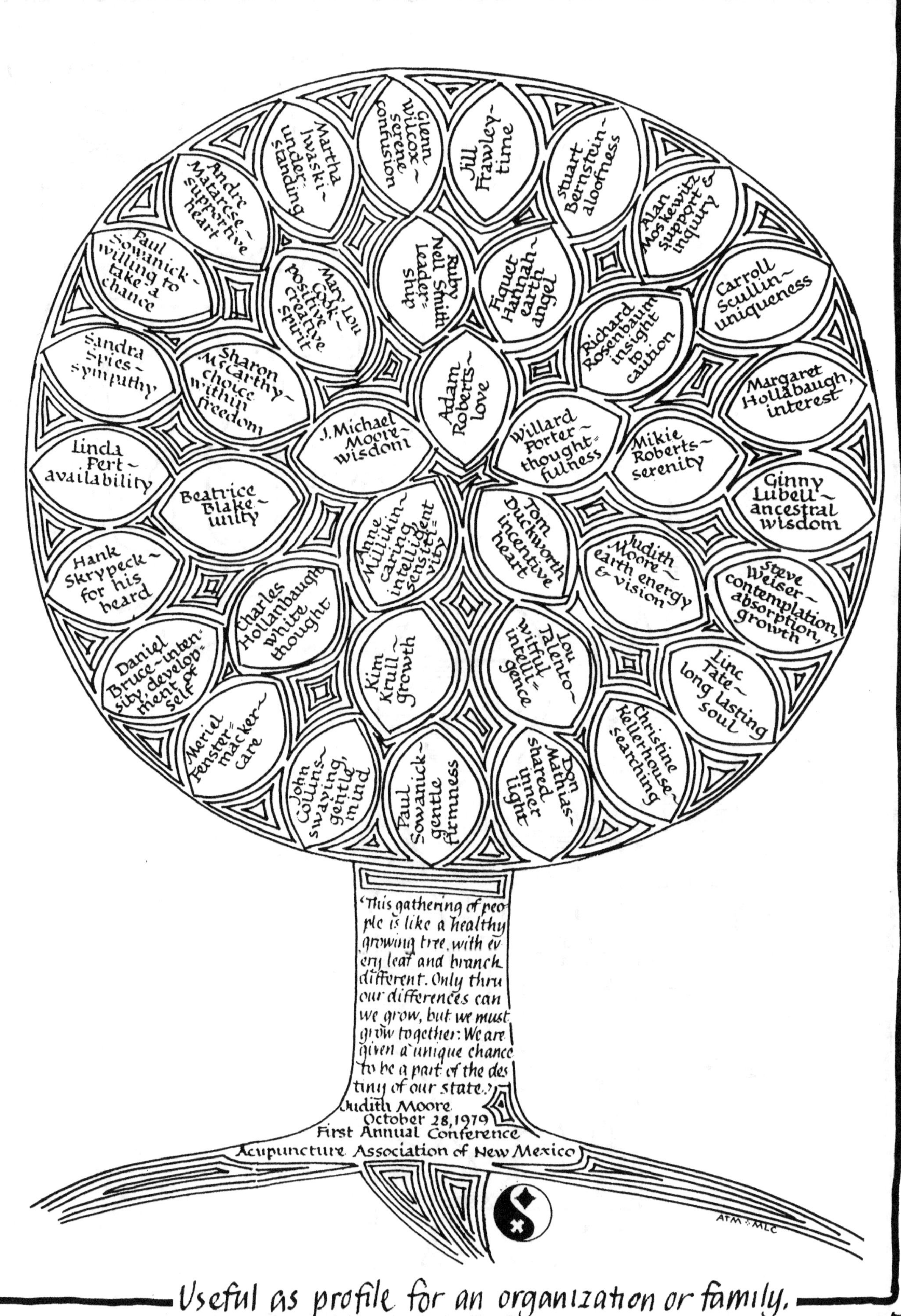

Useful as profile for an organization or family.

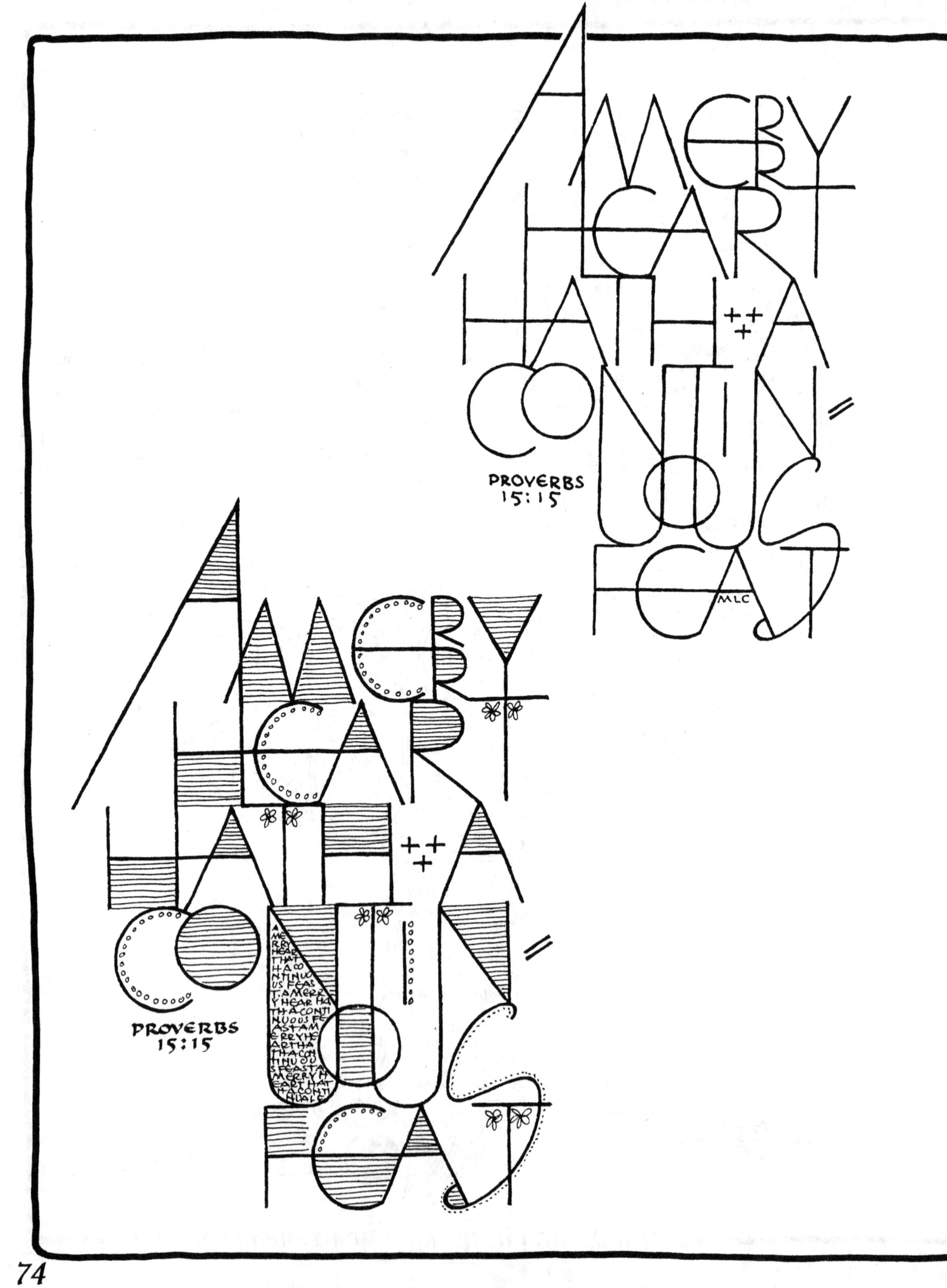
PROVERBS
15:15
MLC
PROVERBS
15:15

I'm putting together a **handbook for peace** & invite you to be part of this project. Your part is to write a simple statement of your thoughts & intentions on peace. Imagine what can happen if enough of us make peace a priority in our lives! Please xerox this page for others, many others. Using an 8½x11" page, draw around your hand. Print your name & address inside the hand, with your statement in the remaining space. Make a copy for yourself, fold the page & mail to me. Thank you for participating.

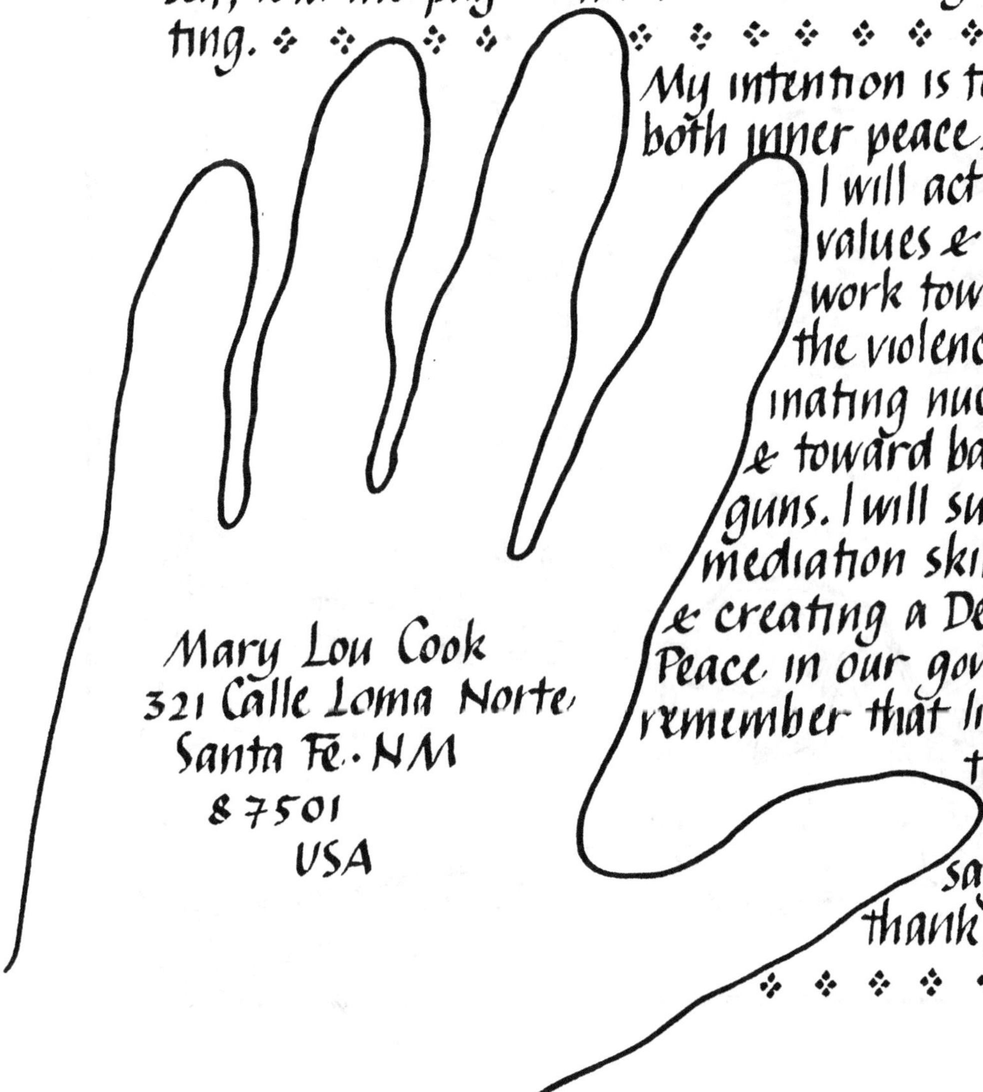

My intention is to work for peace, both inner peace & world peace. I will act on my spiritual values & ideals. I will work toward stopping the violence, toward eliminating nuclear weapons, & toward banishing hand guns. I will support teaching mediation skills in all arenas, & creating a Department of Peace in our government. I will remember that life is precious, that we all are brothers, & to say thank you, thank you, thank you.

Mary Lou Cook
321 Calle Loma Norte
Santa Fe · NM
87501
USA

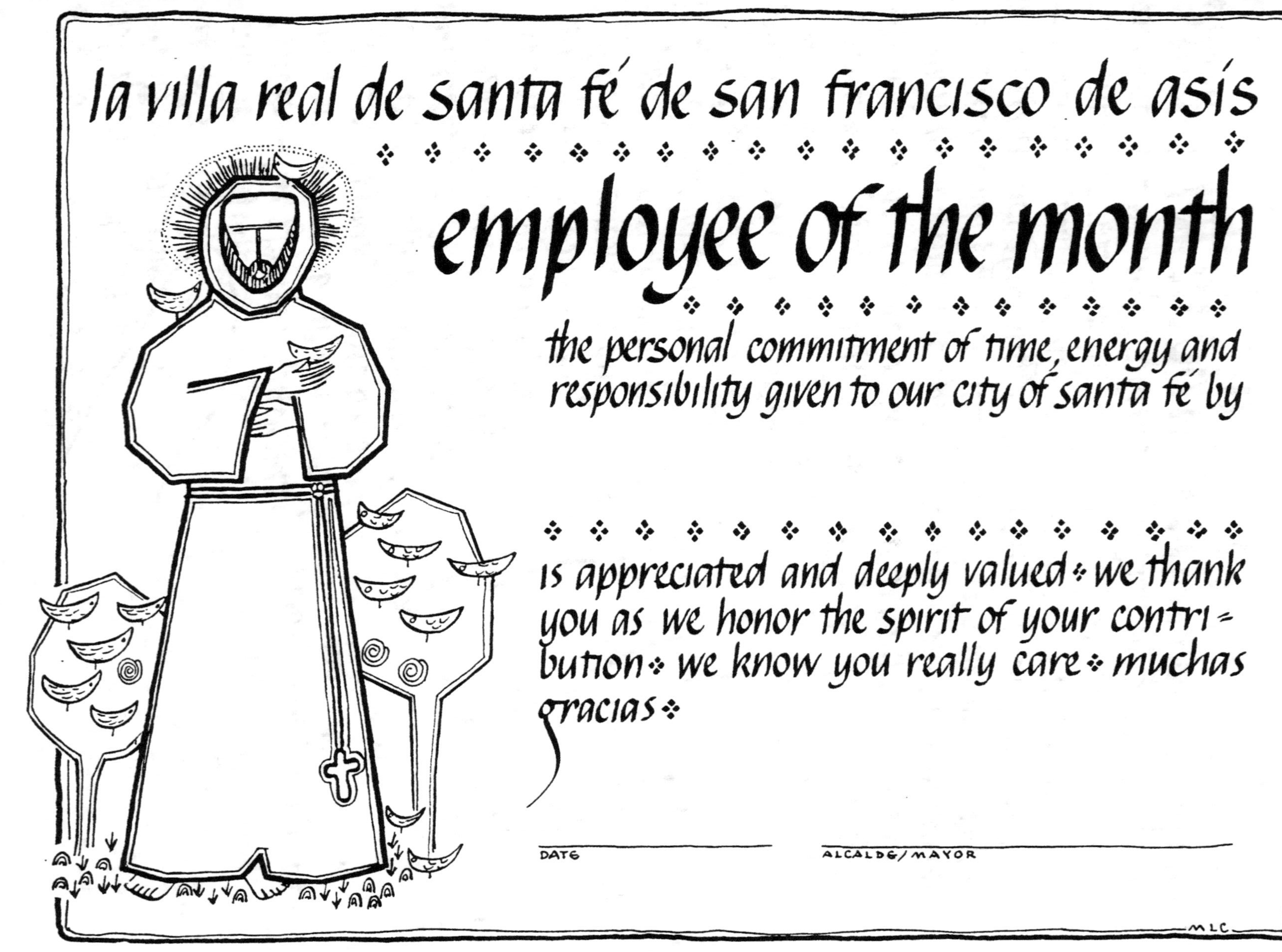

I served as 'Official Calligrapher' for the City of Santa Fe.

TO·SEE·A·WORLD
IN·A·GRAIN·OF·SAND
AND·A·HEAVEN·IN·A
WILD·FLOWER·
HOLD·INFINITY·IN
THE·PALM·OF·YOUR
HAND·AND·ETERNITY
IN·AN·HOUR·

WILLIAM BLAKE

MLC

love is
the inner desire
to return to
the one source

MASAHILO NAKAZONO

MLC

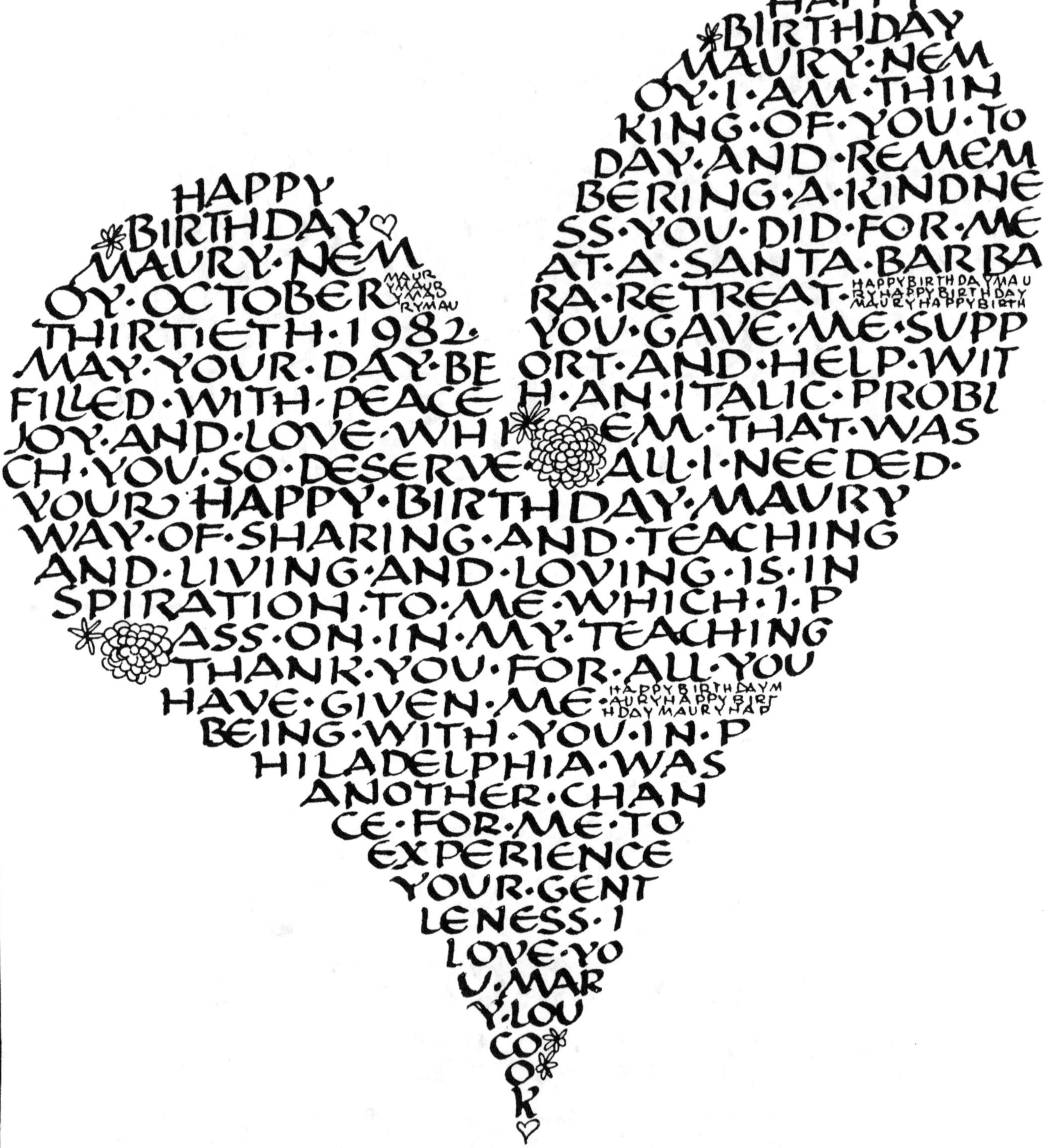

HAPPY
BIRTHDAY
MAURY·NEM
OY·OCTOBER MAUR YMAUR YMAU RYMAU
THIRTIETH·1982·
MAY·YOUR·DAY·BE
FILLED·WITH·PEACE
JOY·AND·LOVE·WHI
CH·YOU·SO·DESERVE·

HAPPY
BIRTHDAY
MAURY·NEM
OY·I·AM·THIN
KING·OF·YOU·TO
DAY·AND·REMEM
BERING·A·KINDNE
SS·YOU·DID·FOR·ME
AT·A·SANTA·BARBA
RA·RETREAT· HAPPYBIRTHDAYMAU RYHAPPYBIRTHDAY MAURYHAPPYBIRTH
YOU·GAVE·ME·SUPP
ORT·AND·HELP·WIT
H·AN·ITALIC·PROBL
EM·THAT·WAS
ALL·I·NEEDED·

YOUR HAPPY·BIRTHDAY·MAURY
WAY·OF·SHARING·AND·TEACHING
AND·LIVING·AND·LOVING·IS·IN
SPIRATION·TO·ME·WHICH·I·P
ASS·ON·IN·MY·TEACHING
THANK·YOU·FOR·ALL·YOU
HAVE·GIVEN·ME· HAPPYBIRTHDAYM AURYHAPPYBIRT HDAYMAURYHAP
BEING·WITH·YOU·IN·P
HILADELPHIA·WAS
ANOTHER·CHAN
CE·FOR·ME·TO
EXPERIENCE
YOUR·GENT
LENESS·I
LOVE·YO
U·MAR
Y·LOU
CO
O
K

hearts are in bloom & welcome every day of the year

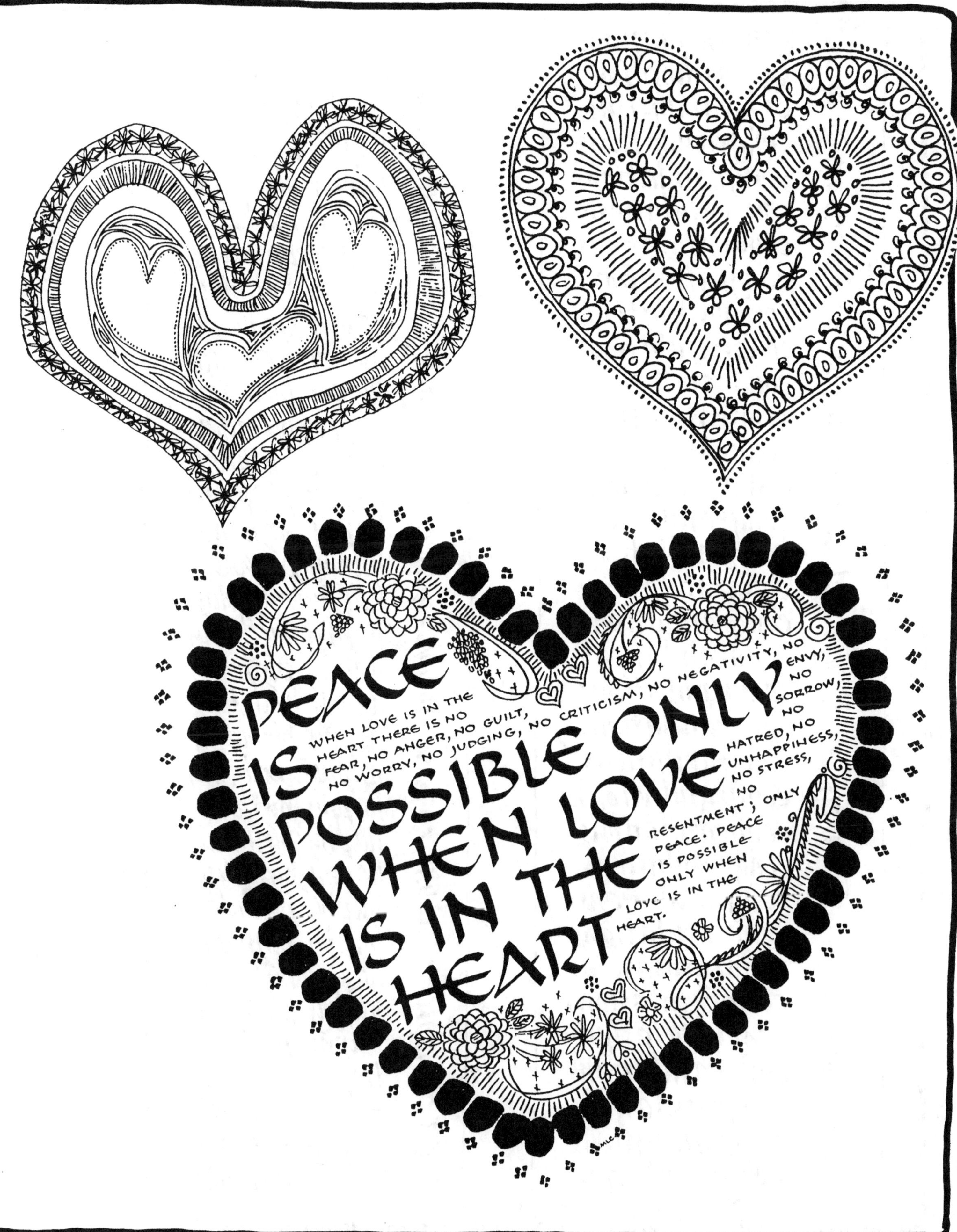
PEACE IS POSSIBLE ONLY WHEN LOVE IS IN THE HEART
WHEN LOVE IS IN THE HEART THERE IS NO FEAR, NO ANGER, NO GUILT, NO WORRY, NO JUDGING, NO CRITICISM, NO NEGATIVITY, NO ENVY, NO SORROW, NO HATRED, NO UNHAPPINESS, NO STRESS, NO RESENTMENT; ONLY PEACE. PEACE IS POSSIBLE ONLY WHEN LOVE IS IN THE HEART.

carroll griesedieck ∴ february 6 · with love + blessings + miracles + rainbows + joy ∴ mlc ♡

congratulations
congratulations
congratulations
congratulations
congratulations
congratulations
congratulations
congratulations
congratulations
congratulations
congratulations
congratulations
congratulations
congratulations
congratulations
congratulations
congratulations
congratulations
congratulations
congratulations
congratulations
congratulations
congratulations
congratulations
congratulations
congratulations
congratulations
congratulations
congratulations
congratulations
congratulations
congratulations
congratulations
congratulations

anita thompson ∴ december 17 ∴ with love + peace + blessings + joy ∴ from mlc ♡

happy birthday
happy birthday
happy birthday
happy birthday
happy birthday
happy birthday
happy birthday
happy birthday
happy birthday
happy birthday
happy birthday
happy birthday
happy birthday
happy birthday
happy birthday
happy birthday
happy birthday
happy birthday
happy birthday
happy birthday
happy birthday
happy birthday
happy birthday
happy birthday
happy birthday
happy birthday
happy birthday
happy birthday
happy birthday
happy birthday
happy birthday
happy birthday
happy birthday

long scrolls with ends rolled around small bamboo·yarn hangers the international women's writing guild is — chrysalis skein of wool circle of mindfulness empowerment of self paradox and — in silent partnership with the spiritual

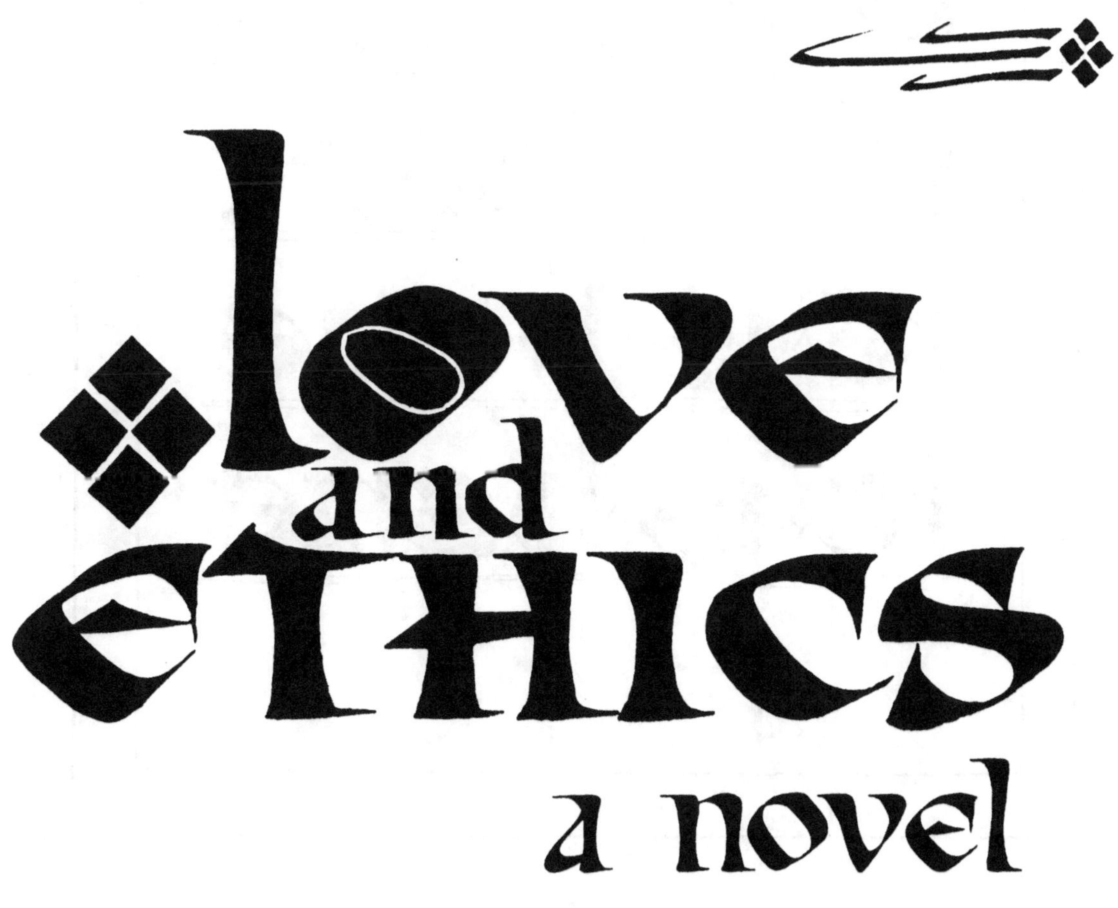

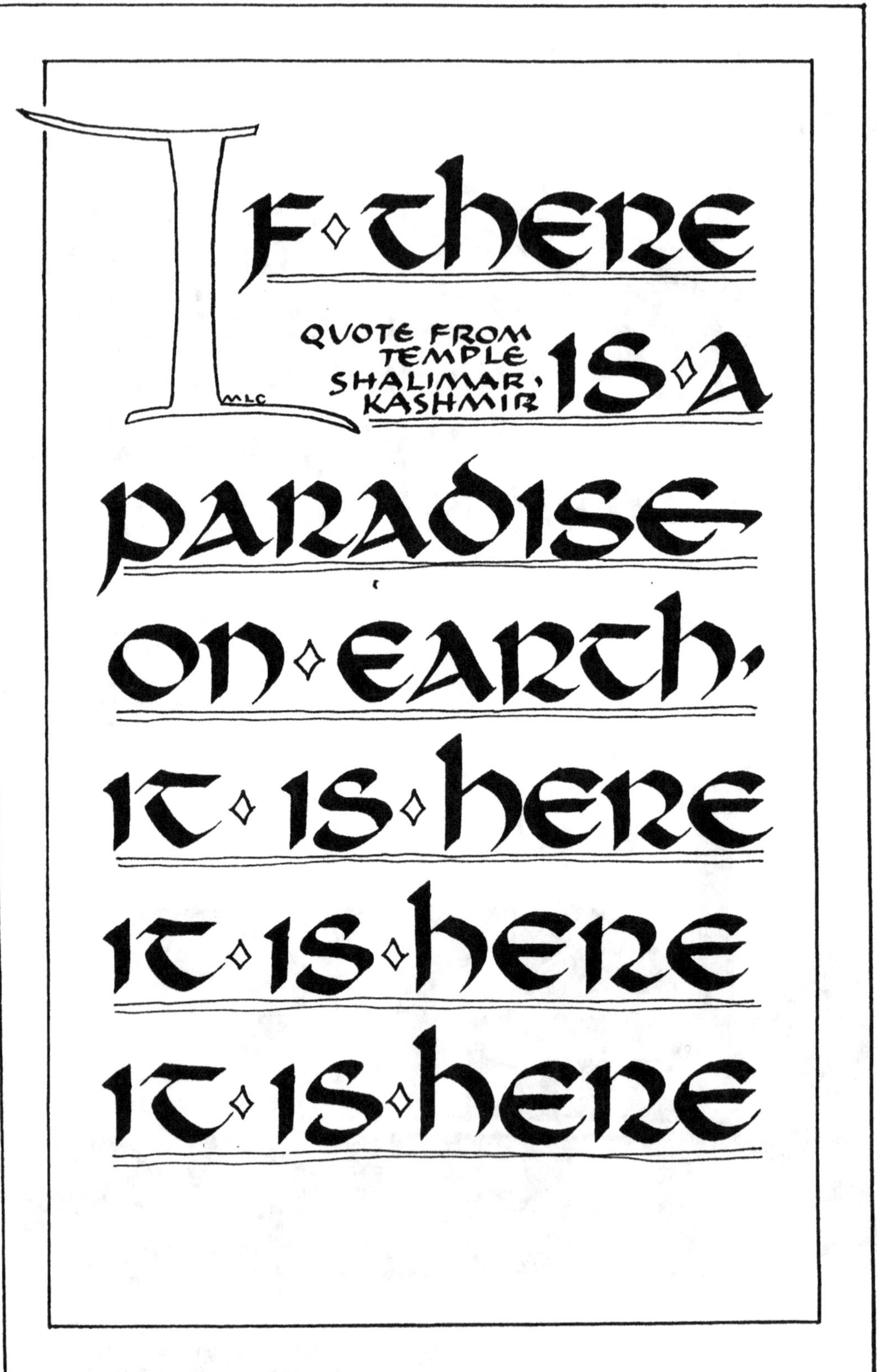

house blessings. with space at bottom for names of occupants & pets

Bless · This · House

Bless those who dwell within, & all who enter. We welcome warm hearts, friends, music, laughter, & tears. May this be a place of sanctuary, peace, harmony & healing. Let our roots grow deep. Amen

scripsit · m. l. · cook

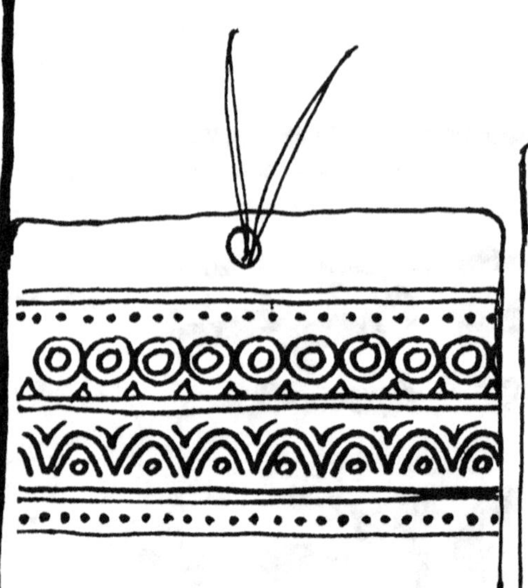

this tree is planted with joy & celebration

this tree is planted in loving memory

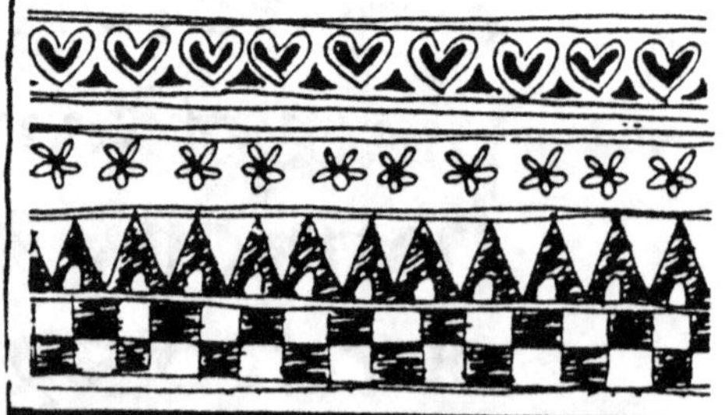

AIDS MEMORIAL GARDEN
4·9·95

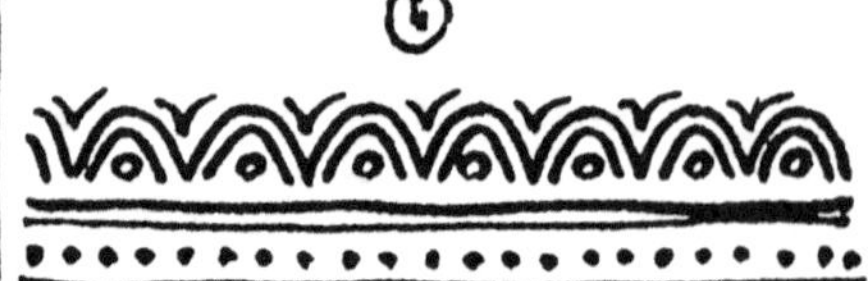

Do not stand at my grave & weep, I am not there. I am a thousand winds that blow. I am the sunlight. I am the gentle autum rain, & I am the soft starlight at night. I am here with the trees, smiling.

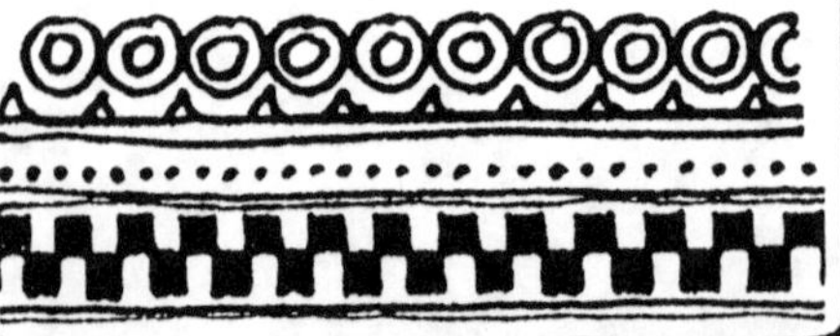

tree notes to hang on branches · print on colored paper

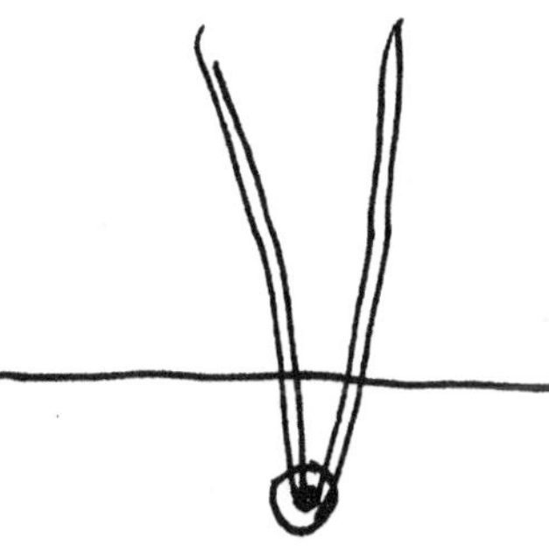

In Honor
and Memory
of
Our Beloved
President
BILL WITTER

A Man of
Nobility
Vision
Courage
and
Love

Santa Fe
Community
College
August 12
1 9 9 3

thank you
thank you
thank you
thank you
thank you
thank you

If the only prayer
you ever give is
"thank you", that
would be enough.
Meister Eckhart

sharron +
mike
7 · 21 · 2001

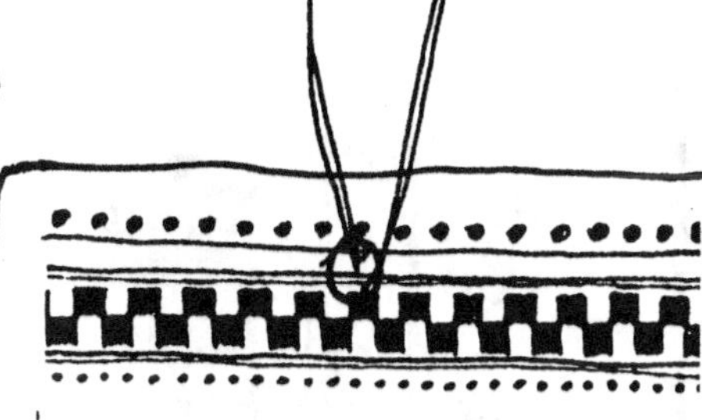

happy birthday
happy birthday
happy birthday
happy birthday
happy birthday
happy birthday
happy birthday
happy birthday
happy birthday
happy birthday
happy birthday
happy birthday
happy birthday
happy birthday
happy birthday
happy birthday
happy birthday
happy birthday
happy birthday
happy birthday

GREEN INK · TREE NOTES ©

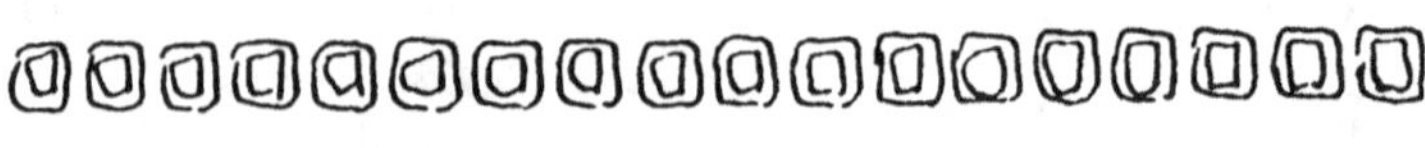

A CERTIFICATE OF OUR
THANKS

WITH ACKNOWLEDGMENT &
GRATEFUL APPRECIATION FROM
THE ALUMNI OF THE SANTA
FE INSTITUTE OF FINE ARTS
TO **JAN LUSTIG**

thank you · thank you · thank you · th
ank you · thank you · thank you · than
k you · thank you · thank you · thank y
ou · thank you · thank you · thank you ·
thank you · thank you · thank you · th
ank you · thank you · thank you · thank
you · muchas gracias · thank you · tha
nk you · thank you · thank you · thank
you · thank you for everything jan

1993

SCRIPSIT MLC

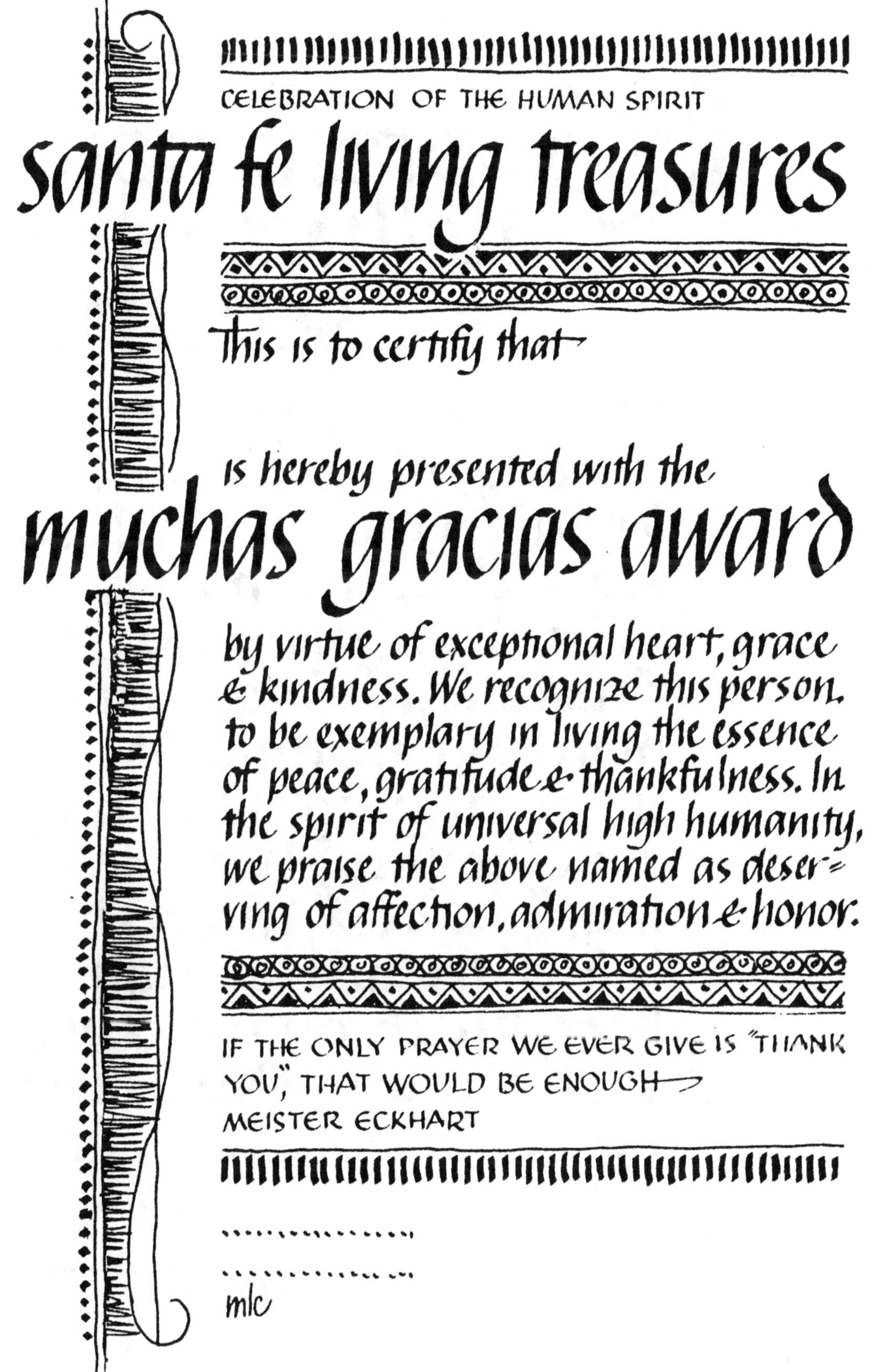
CELEBRATION OF THE HUMAN SPIRIT
santa fe living treasures
this is to certify that
is hereby presented with the
muchas gracias award
by virtue of exceptional heart, grace & kindness. We recognize this person to be exemplary in living the essence of peace, gratitude & thankfulness. In the spirit of universal high humanity, we praise the above named as deserving of affection, admiration & honor.
IF THE ONLY PRAYER WE EVER GIVE IS "THANK YOU", THAT WOULD BE ENOUGH
MEISTER ECKHART
mlc

In appreciation of melba & john schlenk

• •

for dog/plant feeding & loving, window washing, stove cleaning, hub cap polishing, furniture re-finishing, gluing, caring, mending, ironing, base-ment tidying, go-fering, time keeping, book-keep-ing, $, camera, entertain-ing of friends & neigh-bors, lunch on the table, & all the nice things you do.. • • • • • • • • • • • • • • • • • •

MARCH 79

DAUGHTER

certificate of appreciation

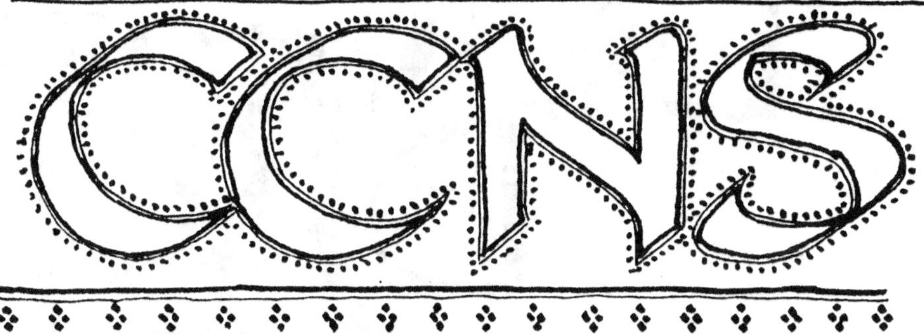

This certificate is to recognize & honor the vision, commitment, energy & courage involved in the founding & direction of Concerned Citizens for Nuclear Safety. Starting in June of 1988, a pattern of integrity & excellence was set by—

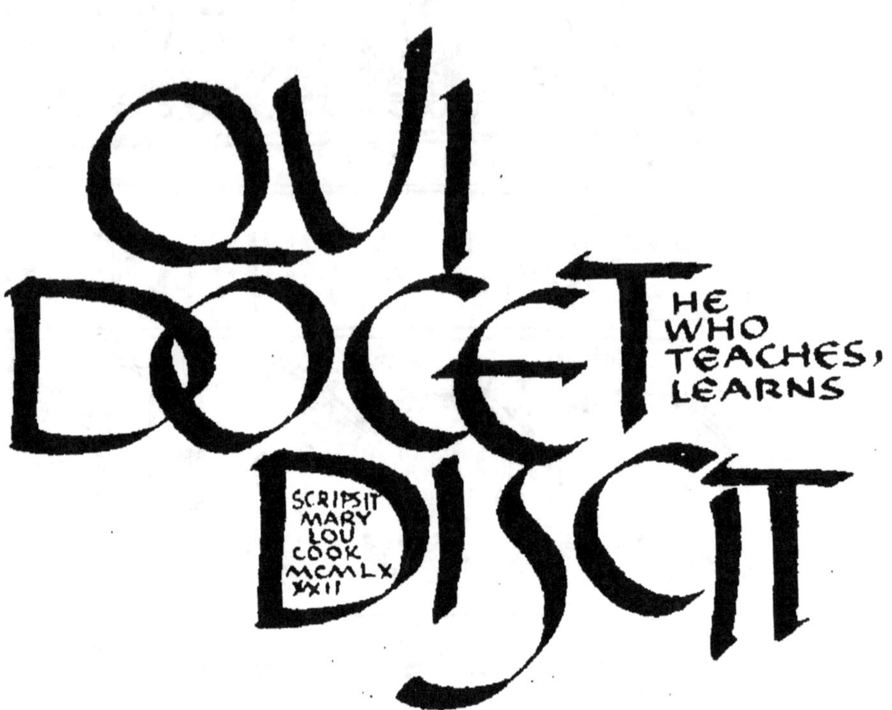
QUI
DOCET
DISCIT
HE WHO TEACHES, LEARNS
SCRIPSIT MARY LOU COOK MCMLXXXII

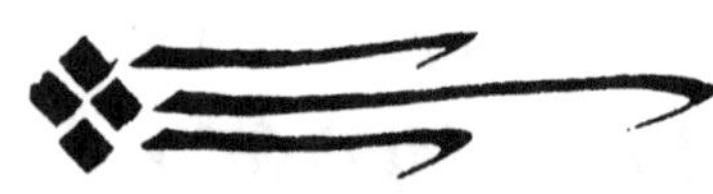

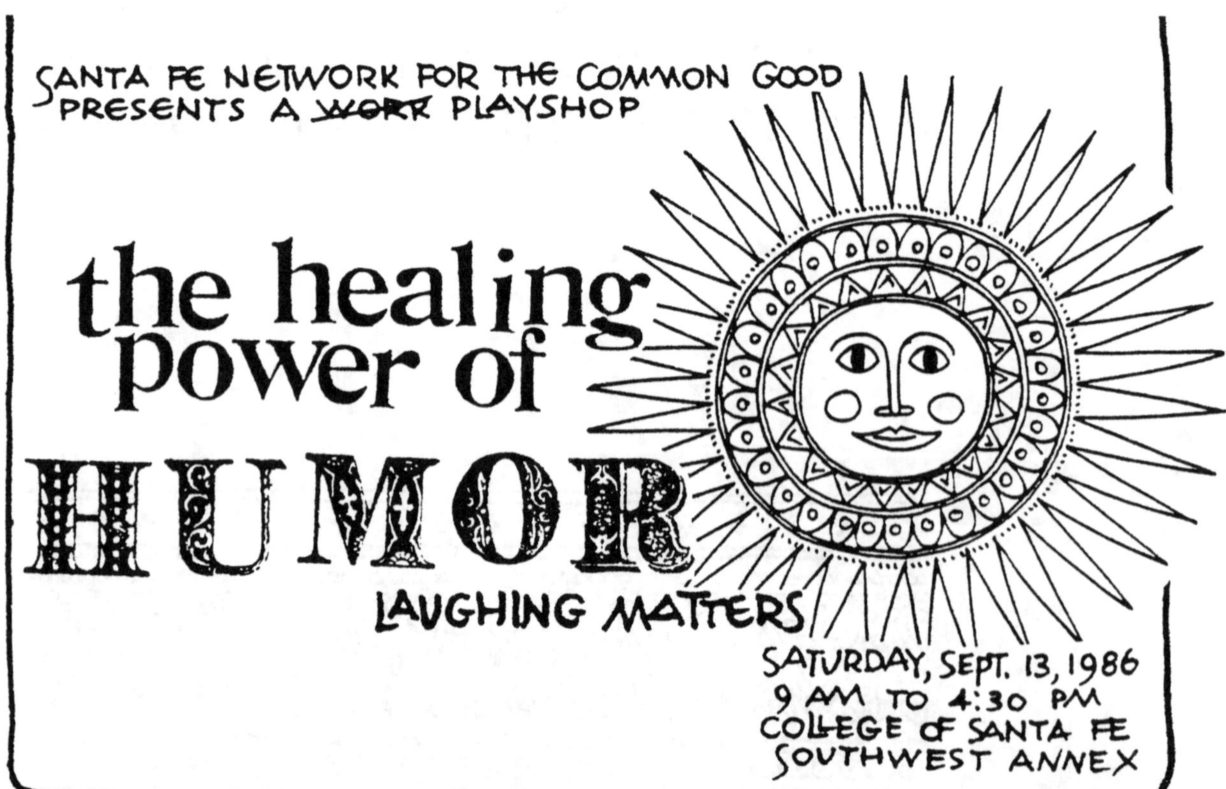
SANTA FE NETWORK FOR THE COMMON GOOD
PRESENTS A WORK PLAYSHOP
the healing power of
HUMOR
LAUGHING MATTERS
SATURDAY, SEPT. 13, 1986
9 AM TO 4:30 PM
COLLEGE OF SANTA FE
SOUTHWEST ANNEX

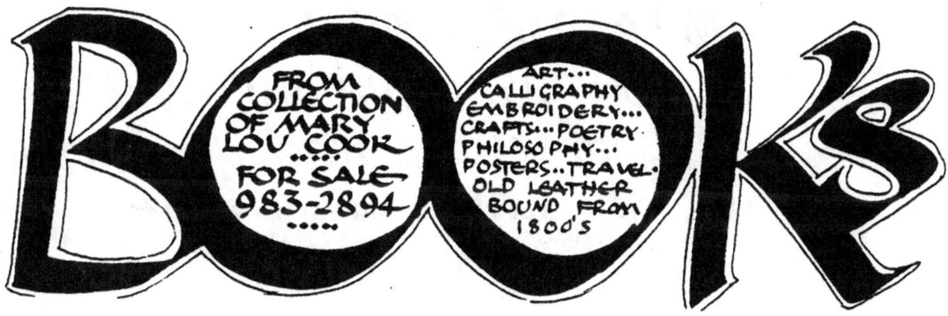
BOOKS
FROM COLLECTION OF MARY LOU COOK
FOR SALE 983-2894
ART... CALLIGRAPHY EMBROIDERY... CRAFTS... POETRY PHILOSOPHY... POSTERS.. TRAVEL. OLD LEATHER BOUND FROM 1800'S

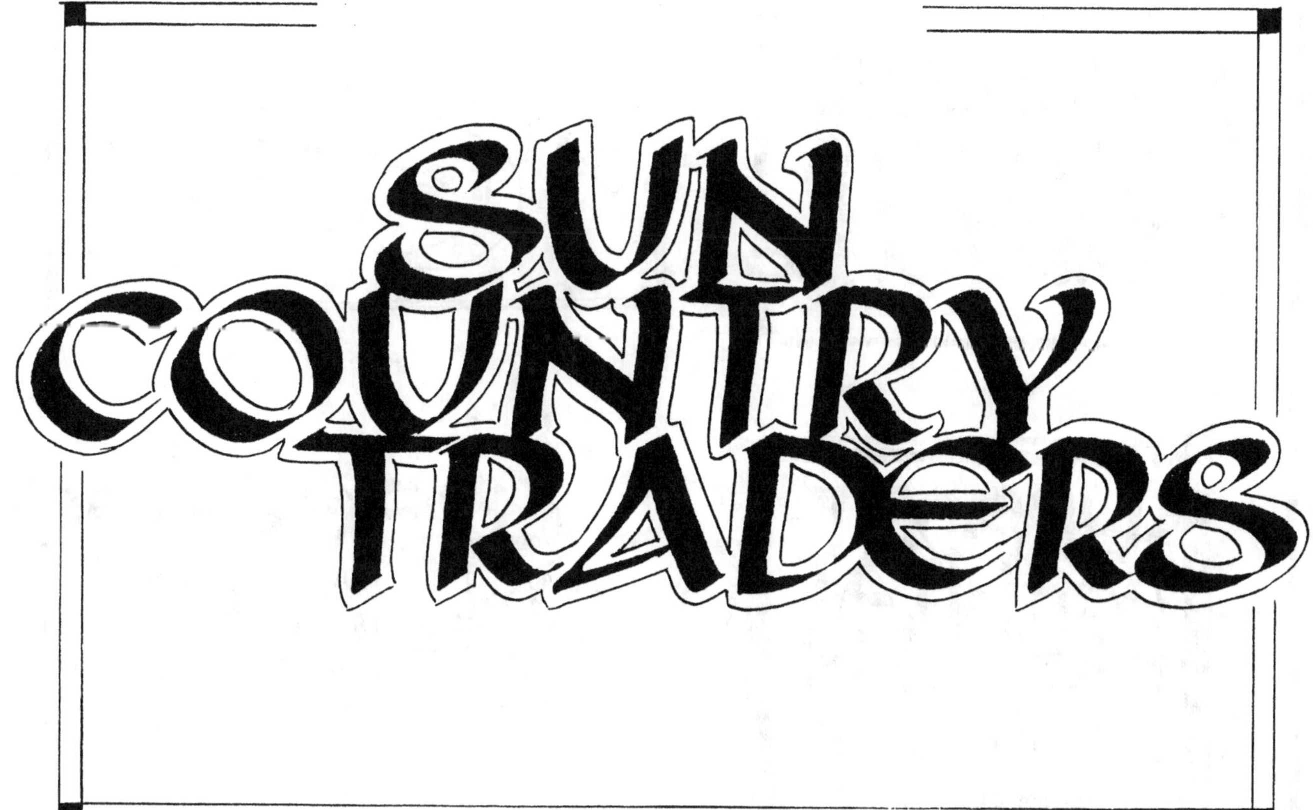
SUN
COUNTRY
TRADERS

violets are red
roses are blue
this valentine's day
i'm wishing for you
a life full of laughter, peace, happiness too
with time for enjoyment of all that you
do ∴ so as i remember good friends such
as vous, i send hugs and this verse
of sentiments true. mary lou cook

321 calle loma norte · santa fe · nm · 87501

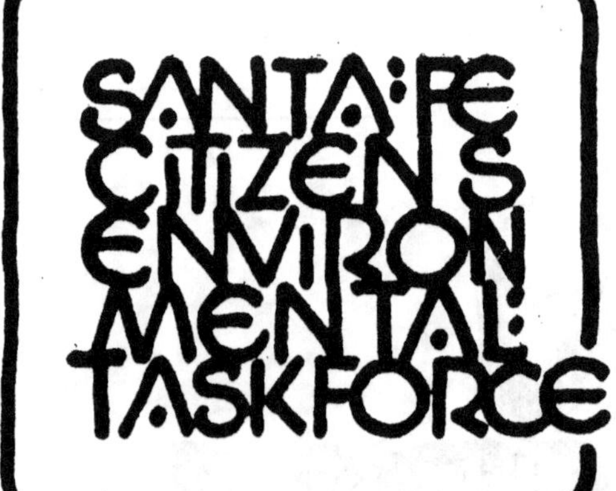

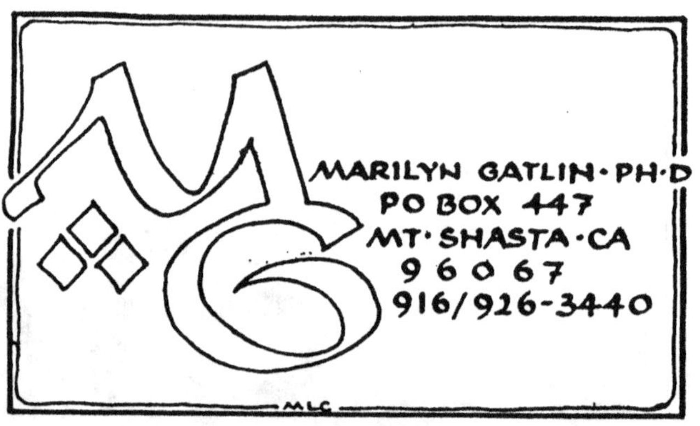

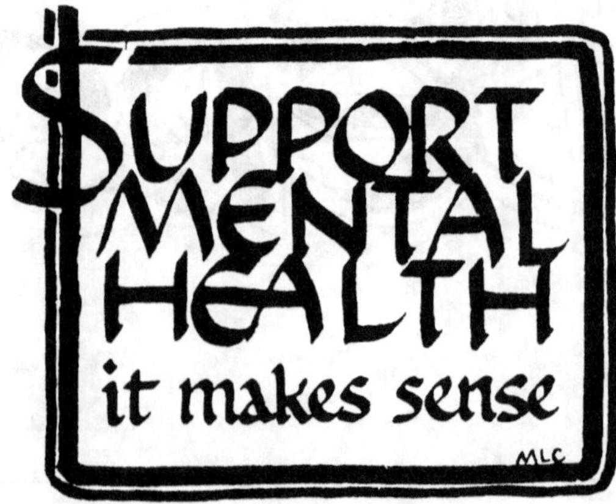

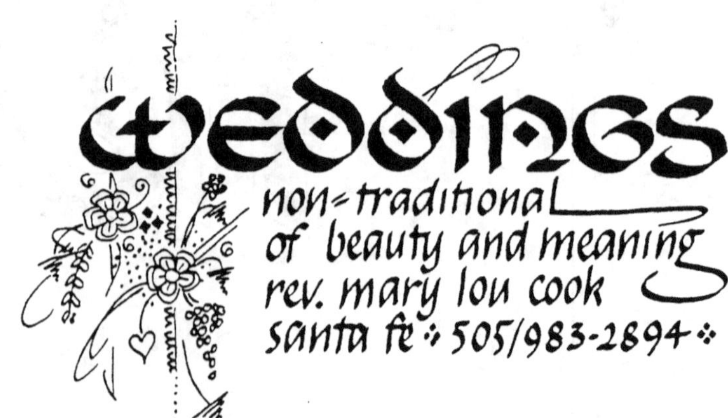

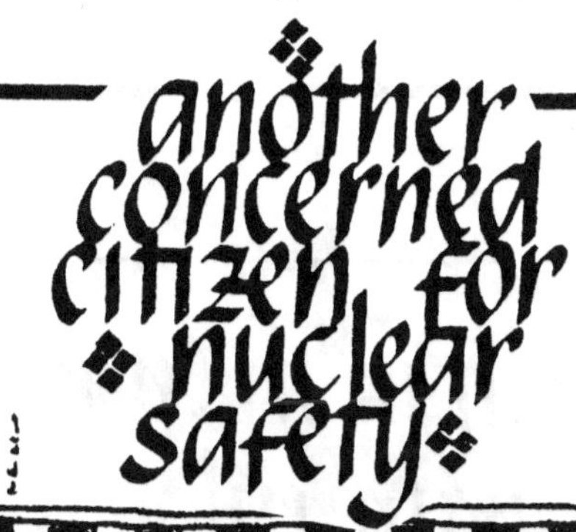

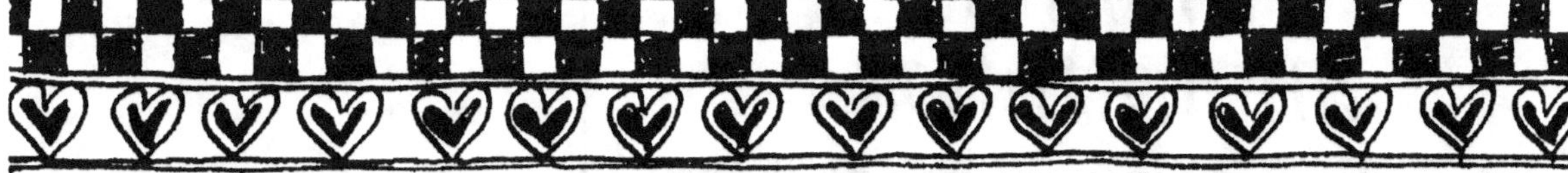

- CALLIGRAPHER
- TREE PLANTER, SANTA FE & KENYA
- TEACHER, LECTURER RE CREATIVITY
- BOOKBINDER, BASKET MAKER
- WORKSHOPS, GETTING ORGANIZED
- COUNSELOR, COURSE IN MIRACLES
- ADVOCATE RE INNER PEACE
- ORDAINED MINISTER & BISHOP, ETERNAL LIFE CHURCH
- INTERNATIONAL WOMEN'S FORUM
- NAMED SANTA FE LIVING TREASURE

MARY LOU COOK

321 CALLE LOMA NORTE
SANTA FE, NEW MEXICO 87501
VOX: 505-983-2894
FAX: 505-983-5828
MLBC@AOL.COM

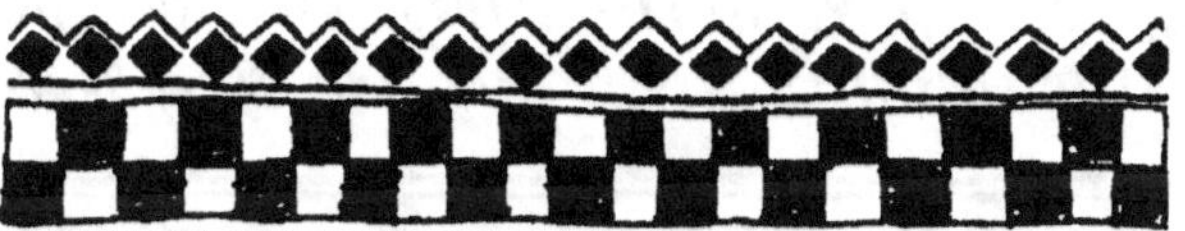

fold the business card

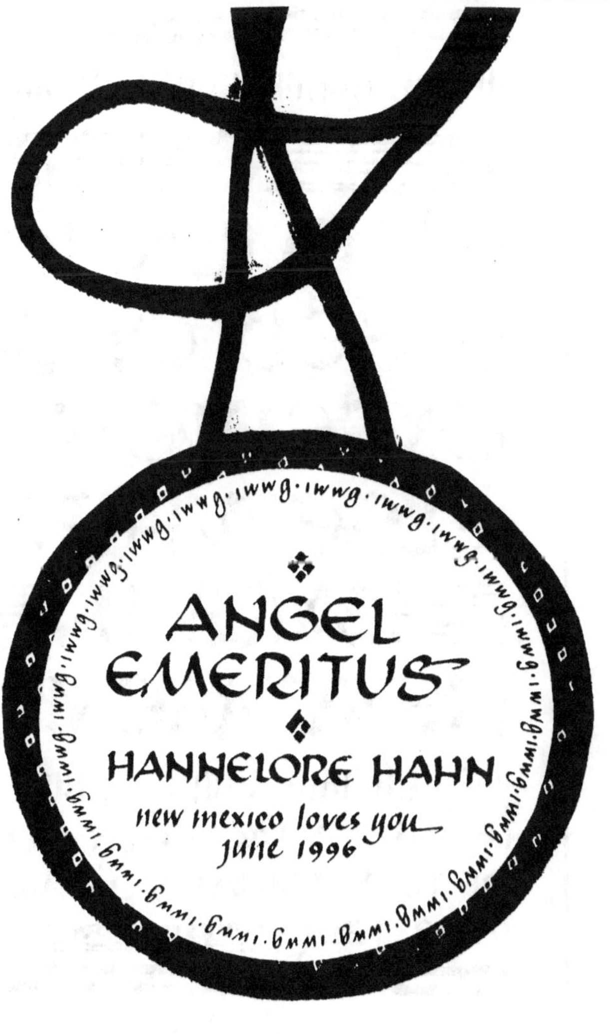

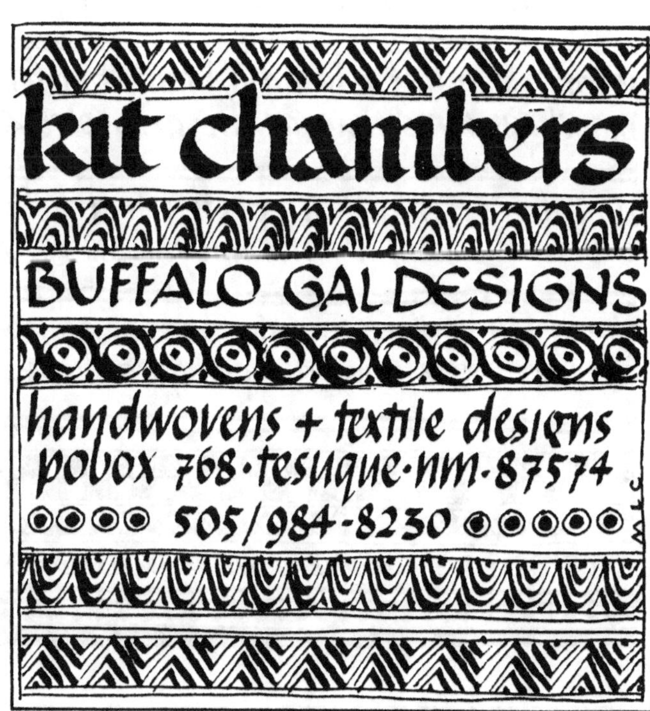

✣ sunday in the park ✣ with mlc an invitation

please come to a celebration of my 80th birthday · all friends in the community & elsewhere are invited · it is my thank you to santa fe ·

sunday, may 3, 1998 · 2:00 in the sam cook grove in devargas park on guadalupe in santa fe · at agua fria ·

plan B: if rain, devargas center at north paseo de peralta

an afternoon of drumming, dancing, poetry, "tatenda*", tree planting, pueblo food, cake, tree notes, love & surprises

come early to watch our skate-boarders

wear a fun hat & bring a blanket or folding chair for sitting on the grass

no gifts — only notes, poetry or art to clip on the long clothes line

mary lou cook · aka mlc · 983-2894

*means "thank you" in Zimbabwe · now an octogeranium

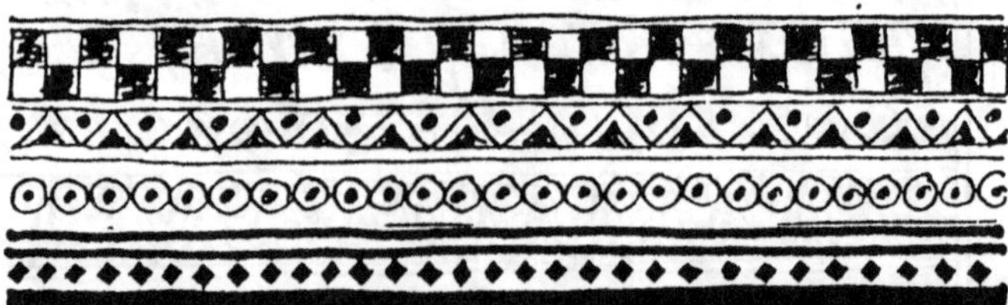

EVERY CALCULATION BASED ON EXPERIENCE ELSEWHERE FAILS IN NEW MEXICO

LEW · A · WALLACE ✣ GOVERNOR OF TERRITORIAL NEW MEXICO 1878-1881 ✣ SCRIPSIT MARY LOU COOK

DEAR◆ROB◆AND◆GEOF
F◆AND◆COLIN◆SUCH◆PL
EASURE◆TO◆HAVE◆YOU
R◆NOTE◆I'M◆BETTER◆TH
ANK◆YOU◆I◆WANT◆TO◆T
ELL◆YOU◆HOW◆MUCH◆I
ENJOY◆WORKING◆WITH
EACH◆OF◆YOU◆AS◆KIN
DRED◆SPIRITS◆IN◆PROT
ECTING◆THE◆PLANET◆T
HERE◆IS◆MUCH◆WORK
TO◆DO◆MY◆HOPE◆IS◆T
HAT◆IT◆IS◆DONE◆IN◆PEA
CE◆RATHER◆THAN◆ANG
ER◆LOVE◆MLC◆♡♡♡♡♡

11·4·2000

please join karla kuyaca, jane shea & mary
lou cook for a reading of karla's work, & to
celebrate her journey to skidmore ∻ we thank
you for your part in this adventure of creativity & trust ∻ wednesday evening, august 7,
7:00 at jane's home, 246 rodriguez ∻ rsvp →
986-9830 or 983-2894 ∻ directions: 1. take east
palace to armijo 2. follow back as far as you
can go on armijo 3. road curves left, continue
until you come to 'dead end' sign 4. right, up
hill about 100 yards, look for 'karla' sign ∻

KARLA

KARLA'S ON HER WAY!

246 rodriguez · santa fe · nm 87501

The Artists of the
Santa Fe Chamber Music Festival
request your company at a Concert honoring
GEORGIA O'KEEFFE
on Saturday, August thirteenth, 1983 ~ 4:00 pm
at the home of Louise Trigg Las Acequias
Nambe, New Mexico

regrets only: 505/455-2562

mc

rt. 1, box 172 · santa fe · nm 87501

'Self-mailers,' eliminating envelopes. Fold so that address shows.

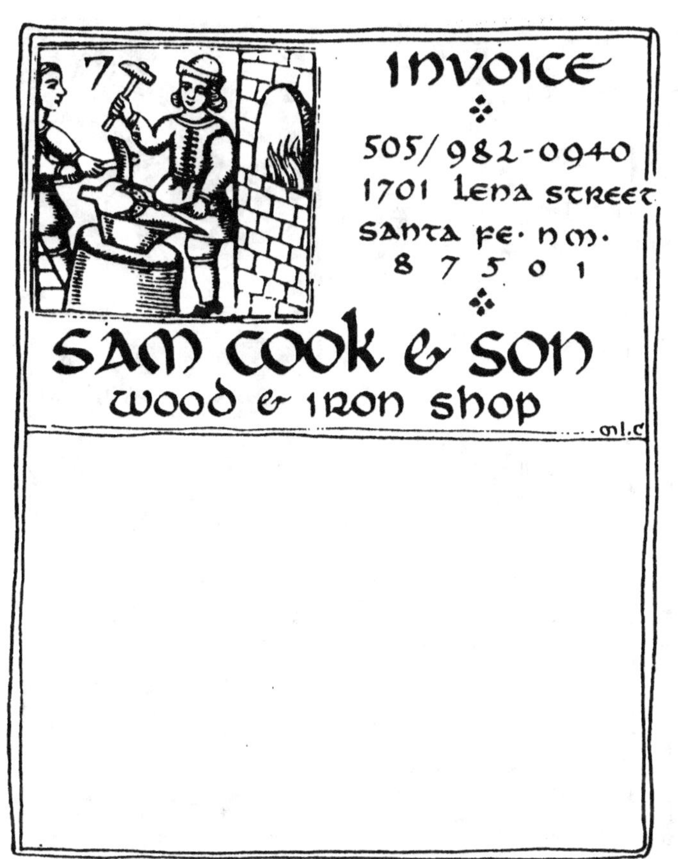

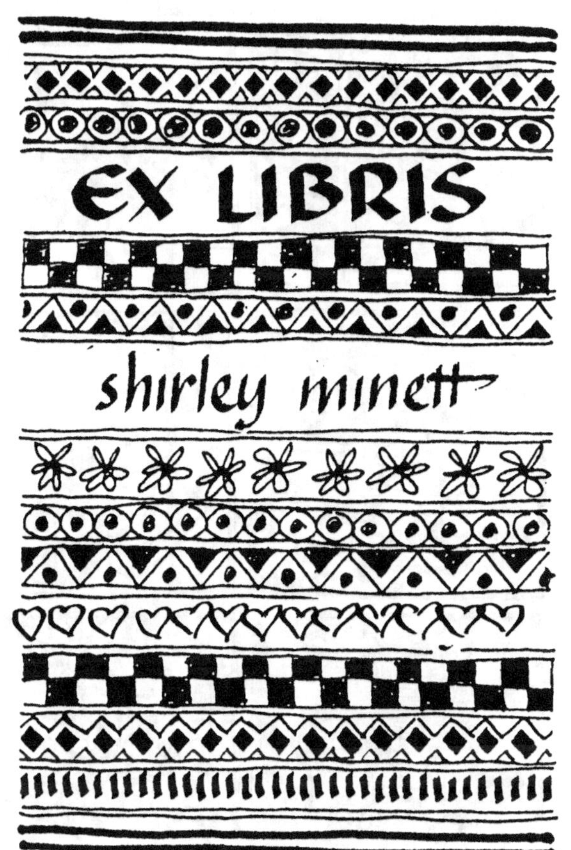

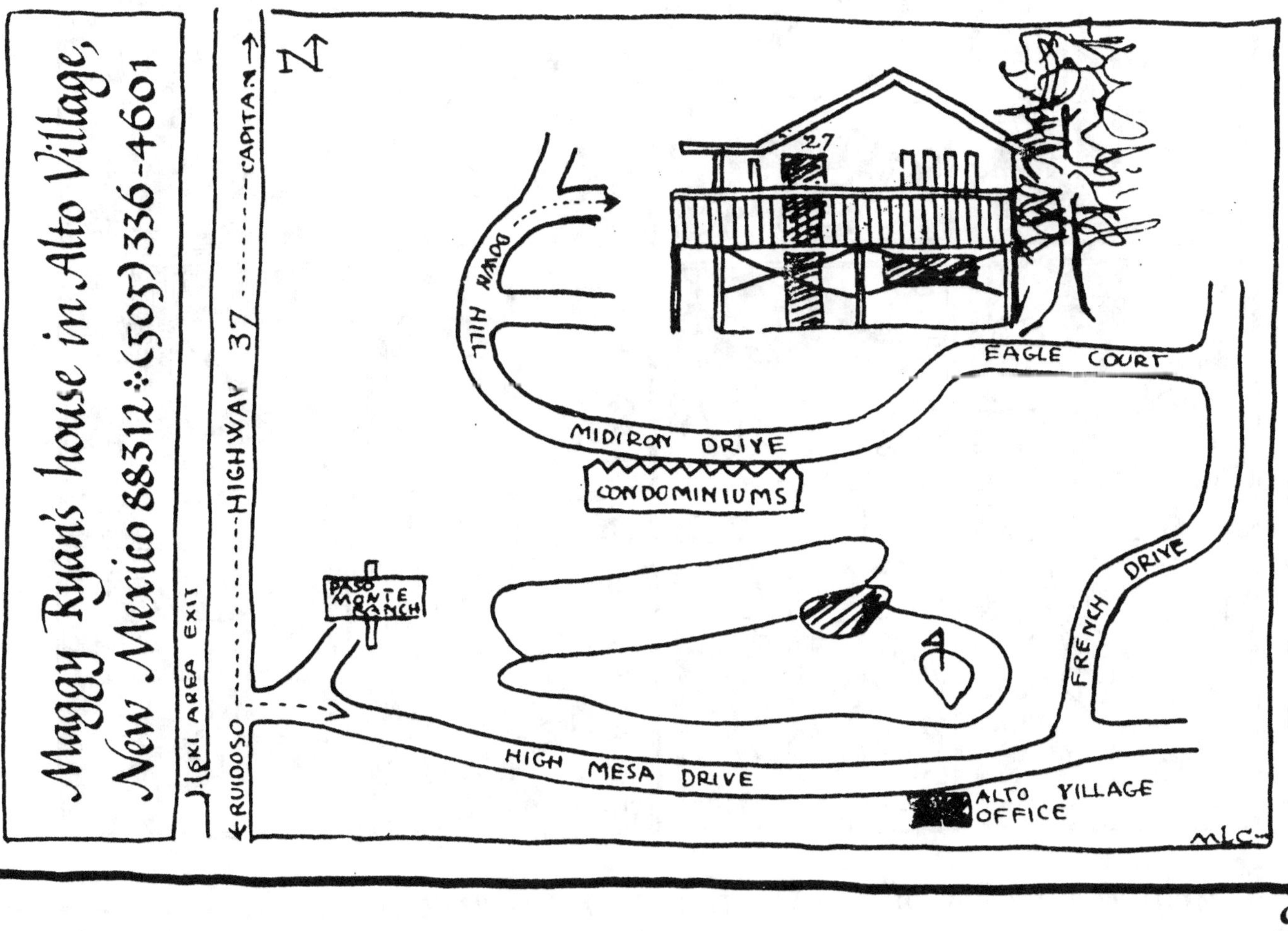

Maggy Ryan's house in Alto Village,
New Mexico 88312 ∻ (505) 336-4601

N
HIGHWAY 37
CAPITAN →
← RUIDOSO
SKI AREA EXIT
PASO MONTE RANCH
HIGH MESA DRIVE
ALTO VILLAGE OFFICE
CONDOMINIUMS
MIDIRON DRIVE
DOWN HILL
EAGLE COURT
FRENCH DRIVE
27
MLC

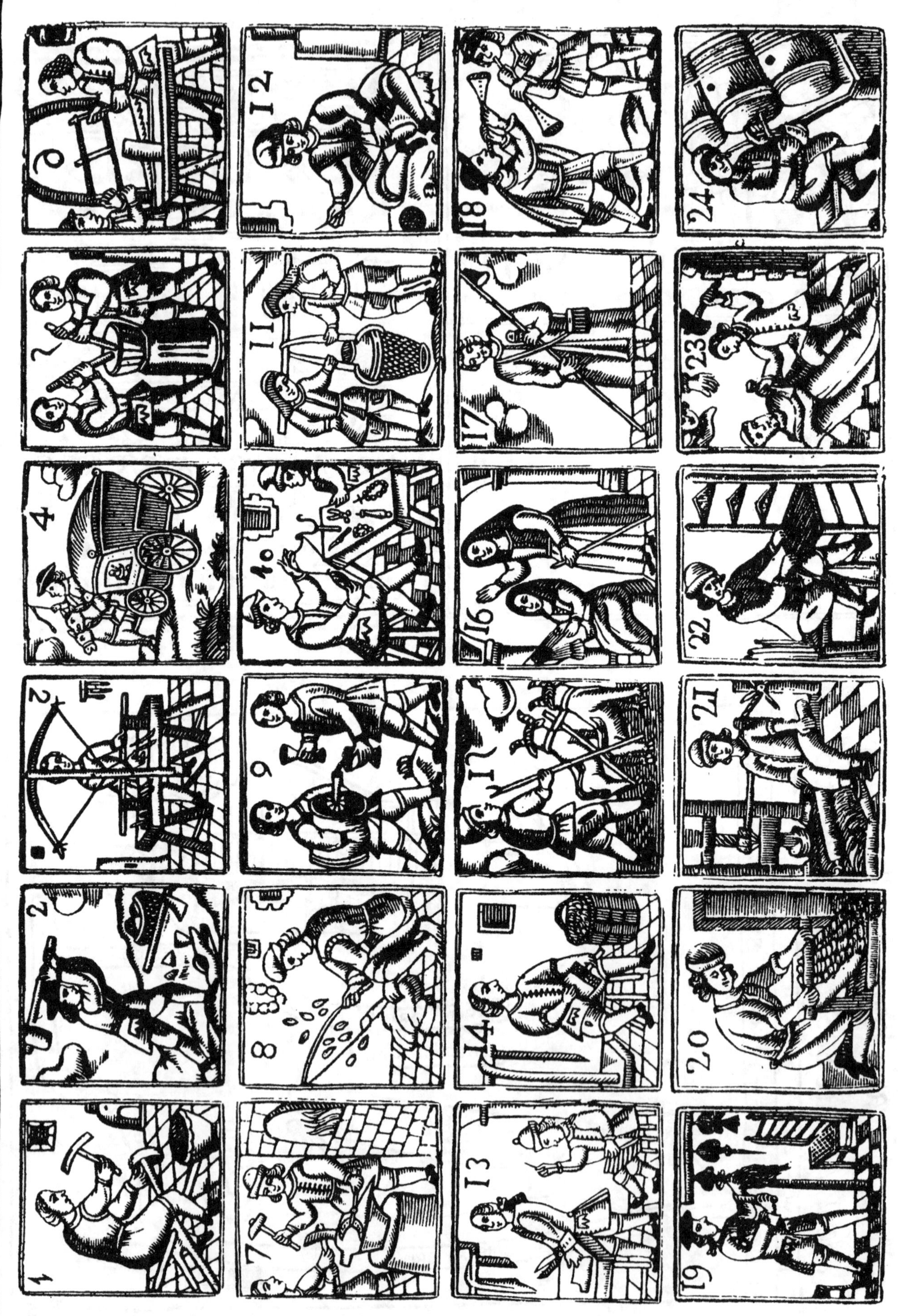

Early wood-cuts of trades found in a Barcelona book store.

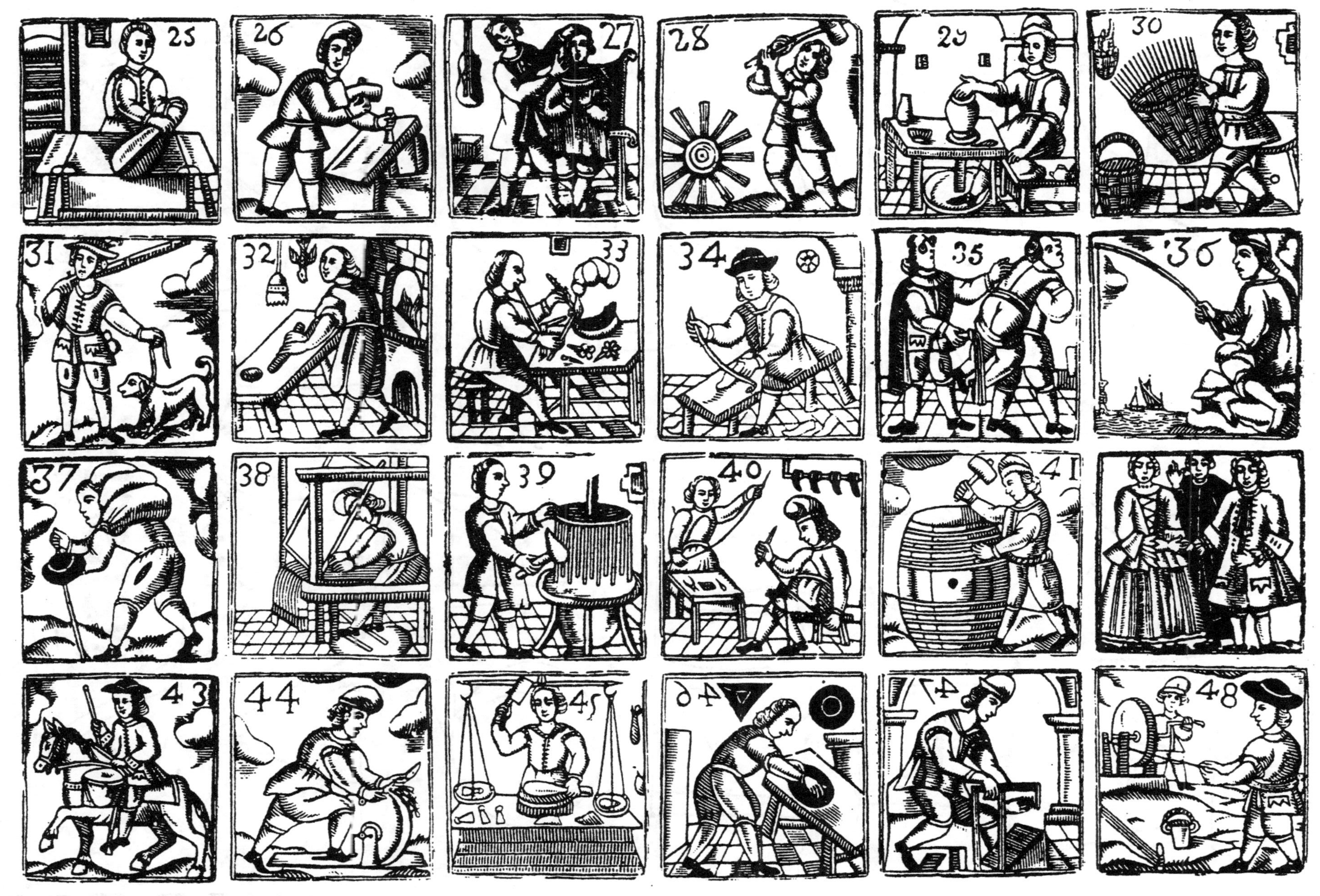

25
26
27
28
29
30
31
32
33
34
35
36
37
38
39
40
41
43
44
45
46
47
48

m.L. cook

VERSALS from book by Oscar Ogg..designed to fit into square shape..for initial use only..

ammo belt holds 'another kind of ammunition'

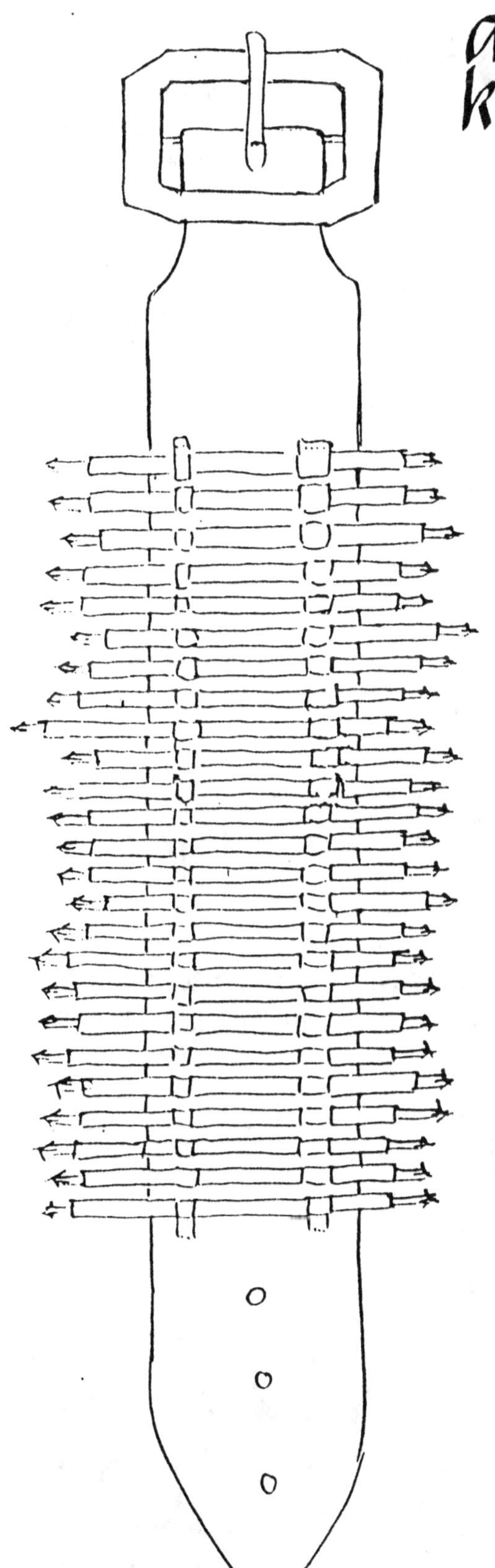

While engaged in my life long addiction, flea marketing, I found an especially great treasure. Indeed, it is so very useful that I'm sharing the idea with design & calligraphy colleagues. This 'find' is a brown leather ammunition belt, as used by cowboys & bad guys of the West, & by soldiers the world over.

And so on a Saturday morning, as I browsed the flea market next to the Santa Fe Opera, which we call 'Der Fliedermarket', this used ammo belt caused my inner alert bells to ring, & I stopped to ponder. As calligraphy is never too far from my senses, I imagined this might be a good pen holder. While pondering, a woman walking by opined that I didn't seem to be the type for an ammo belt. I assured her that I'm not into guns, & that this would be used for something more beneficial to mankind & happiness.

Now with the ammo belt hung on the wall by my writing desk, I'm a happy advocate of this organized pen holder. There are 25 small leather loops to hold my Heintze & Blanckertz two sided pen staffs, which provide 50 pen nibs to choose from. I've told design friends of this idea, as they can keep pencils, paint brushes & chop sticks for orderly studio use.

To conclude, 'Another Kind of Ammunition' which comes from our pens is that of beauty, pleasure, inspiring thoughts, communication & words from the heart. In fact, calligraphy is a healthy addiction that could increase writing skills of everyone in this country.

mary lou cook · santa fe · new mexico

mary lou cook · 321 calle loma norte · santa fe · nm 87501

italic handwriting

, called 'everyman's art,' is efficient & practical for everyday use. the 'veriest beginner' will find it easy to learn, & may decide to make it a lifelong skill. this handwriting system is simple & legible, & we hope this basic hand will someday be taught in all schools. For those wanting to develop calligraphic skills, this gives a foundation for making Italic & Roman letterforms with the broad-edged pen. It doesn't take long to learn this beautiful slanted hand & to experience the joy of writing. It gives an eye for good design, an innate sense of visual order & beauty, & evokes self-esteem.

To begin, use a monoline instrument, such as pencil or fine felt pen. Use ruled guide sheet underneath plain bond paper, secured with 2 paper clips. Always warm up with border designs to get hand limber. A slanted lettering board in lap gives optimum results. Lower case letters slant to right, using guide sheet for reference. Letters are crowded, with small space between words, & no loops. Consistency in slant & spacing is important. Be sure that letters touch top & bottom of guide lines. A wedge is created by springing from center of writing line, in 11 letters: a, b, d, g, h, m, n, p, q, r, & u. Heighth of 't' is shorter than other ascenders. After practice, letters can be connected in a cursive mode.

border designs

ilj · nmrhuy · oce · adgq · bptfs · kvwxz

1 2 3 4 5 6
7 8 9 0

Capital letters are somewhat higher than lower case. they can be slanted or straight, but must be consistent. Slanted capitals are narrow, straight capitals are wider. Keep an idea book, & remember that letters need to be lovingly written.

IO · AVHNTZKXYBPR
LEFJSMWOQCGGEUD

IO · AVHNTZXYBP
RLEFJSMWOQC
GGEUD ·

AMPERSANDS

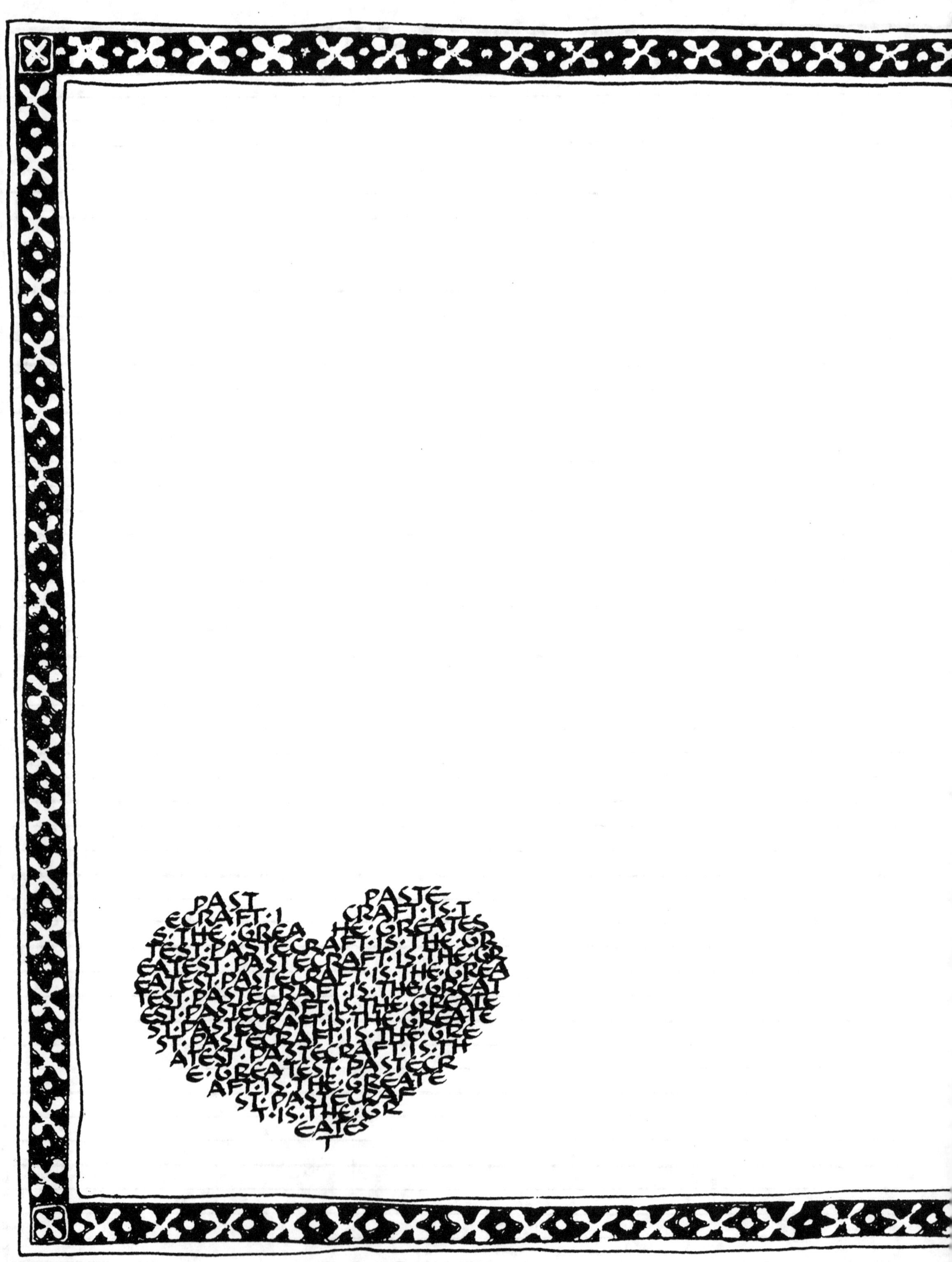
PAST PASTE
ECRAFT·I CRAFT·IS·T
S·THE·GREA HE·GREATES
TEST·PASTECRAFT·IS·THE·GR
EATEST·PASTECRAFT·IS·THE·GR
EATEST·PASTECRAFT·IS·THE·GREA
TEST·PASTECRAFT·IS·THE·GREAT
EST·PASTECRAFT·IS·THE·GREATE
ST·PASTECRAFT·IS·THE·GREATE
ST·PASTECRAFT·IS·THE·GRE
ATEST·PASTECRAFT·IS·TH
E·GREATEST·PASTECR
AFT·IS·THE·GREATE
ST·PASTECRAF
T·IS·THE·GR
EATES
T

Afterword

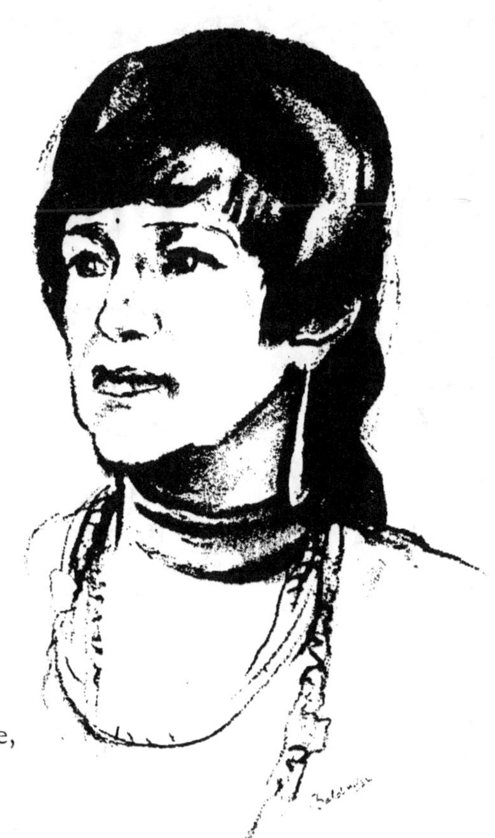

Mary Lou Cook *is a celebrant.*

She celebrates spirit.

In an official capacity, as an ordained minister, MLC leads spiritual ceremonies, especially weddings. The artistic spirit of all the students she encounters is encouraged through the variety of classes she teaches in calligraphy, bookbinding, basketmaking, pastecraft, cross stitch, and organization. People she has not met are also touched through the books she has authored or co-authored on grieving, divorce, humor and Living Treasures.

She celebrates lives.

MLC initiated a program in Santa Fe to recognize the wisdom, accomplishments, and value of chosen elders of the community. This Living Treasures program has spread through the country and the world with information and encouragement supplied by MLC.

Her volunteer activism in Milwaukee, El Paso, Des Moines, Kansas City and in her home of the past 33 years, Santa Fe, has always had a focus on honoring the possibilities of our youth. MLC has been involved with teaching, mentoring, and with facilitating programs in art and multicultural learning.

Planting trees and guarding other living things from environmental threats also occupy her time.

Family, for MLC, has expanded beyond the three beloved children born to her and her late husband, Sam, to include exchange students and numerous others who have found a home with MLC. Her great energy, tempered but not diminished by a long standing diagnosis of leukemia, reflects her enthusiasm for living.

She celebrates creativity.

Through simplicity of design and technique, MLC brings forth a complexity of results in her teaching. Students of varied backgrounds find their own creativity and joy with MLC's nudging.

Her respect for folk art has been nurtured by her travels for peace to Africa, Europe, and Mexico and by her work with the Peace Corps and AFS International Scholarships.

Her lifelong fascination with letters has been made visible in her work as a professional scribe. Calligraphy and pastecraft adhere to each other here in a natural alliance, arts of every person.

This book of Pastecraft is Mary Lou Cook's invitation to join in the celebration.

—Kathy Chilton, Albuquerque

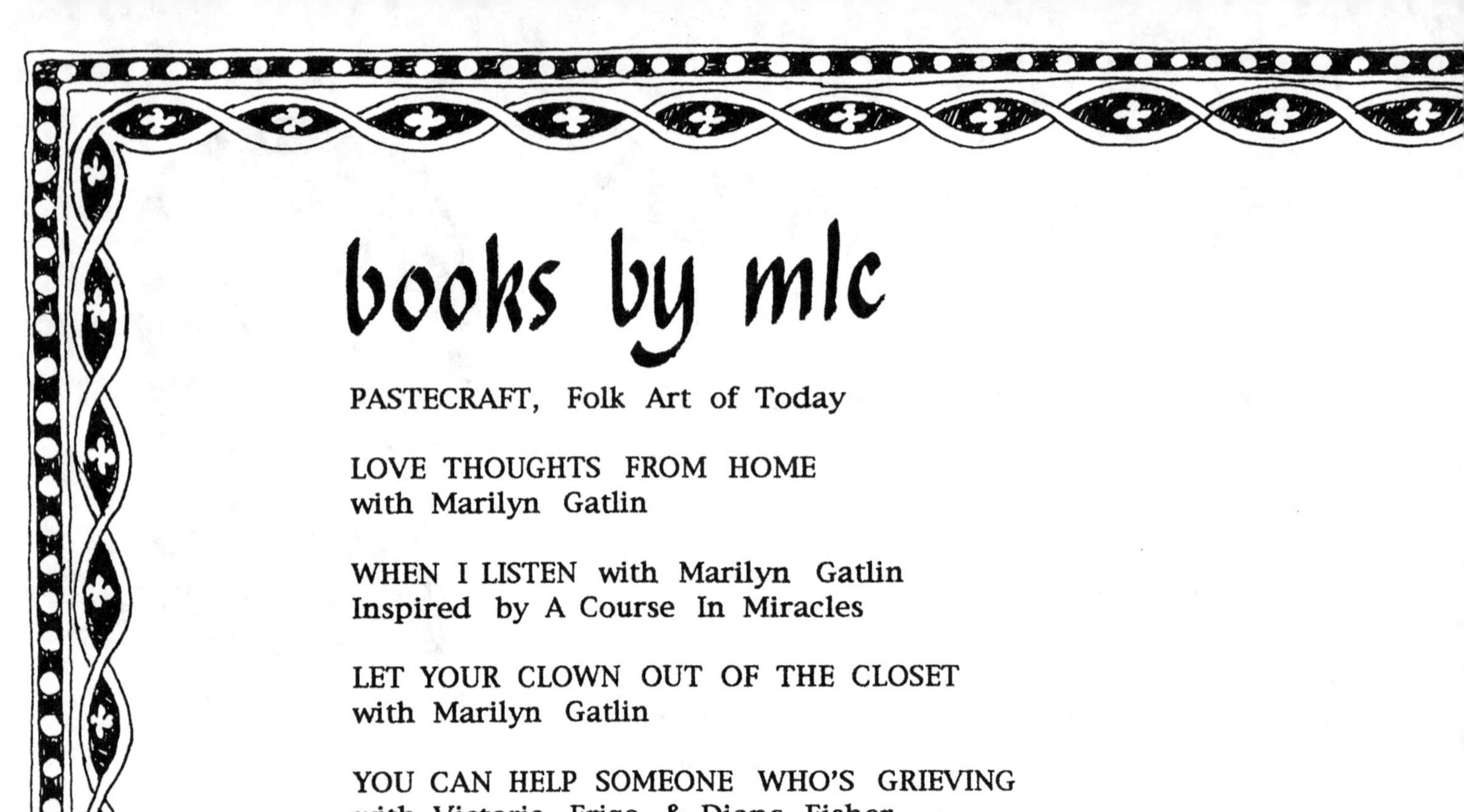

books by mlc

PASTECRAFT, Folk Art of Today

LOVE THOUGHTS FROM HOME
with Marilyn Gatlin

WHEN I LISTEN with Marilyn Gatlin
Inspired by A Course In Miracles

LET YOUR CLOWN OUT OF THE CLOSET
with Marilyn Gatlin

YOU CAN HELP SOMEONE WHO'S GRIEVING
with Victoria Frigo & Diane Fisher

OPEN ENDINGS, After Divorce & Other Changes
with Jan Boyer

BOOK OF A, with Scribes Eight

LIVING TREASURES
Celebration of the Human Spirit
with Karen Brandt & Sharon Niederman
* to order send $4 priority mail

LIVING TREASURES HOW-TO HANDBOOK
Starting this program in your community

PORTFOLIO OF FOLK ART PATTERNS, #1
International Folk Art Museum, Santa Fe
with Winifred Bream, Carol Steiro & Leigh Peacock

PORTFOLIO OF FOLK ART PATTERNS, #2
International Folk Art Museum, Santa Fe
with Winifred Bream, Carol Steiro & Leigh Peacock

♦♦♦♦

These books available directly from the author.
321 Calle Loma Norte, Santa Fe, NM 87501
505/983-2894 fax: 505/983-5828 mlbc@aol.com
http://members.aol.com/mlbc wwwlivingtreasures.kxx.com

live in joy
even
though you have all the facts

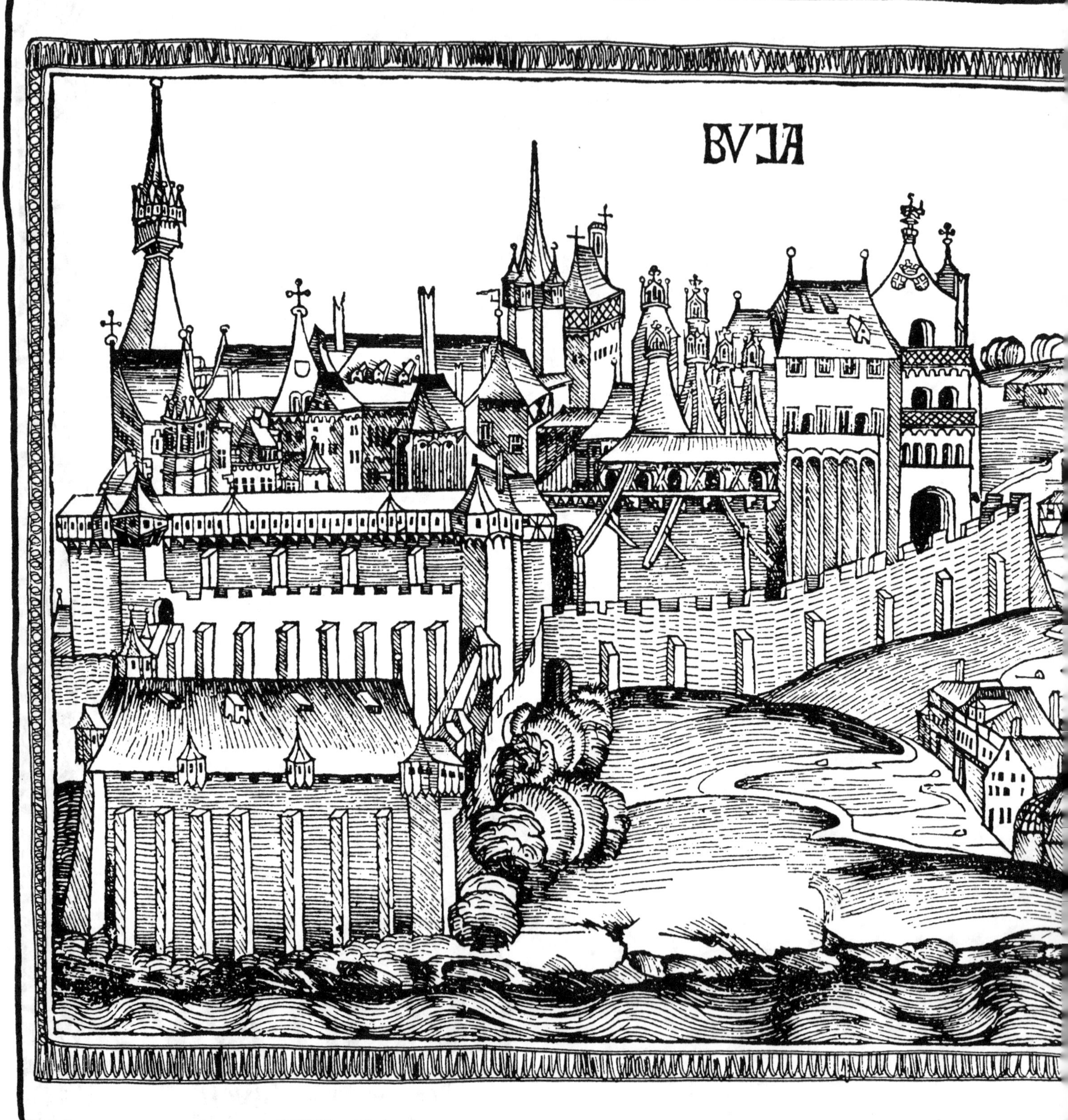
BVDA

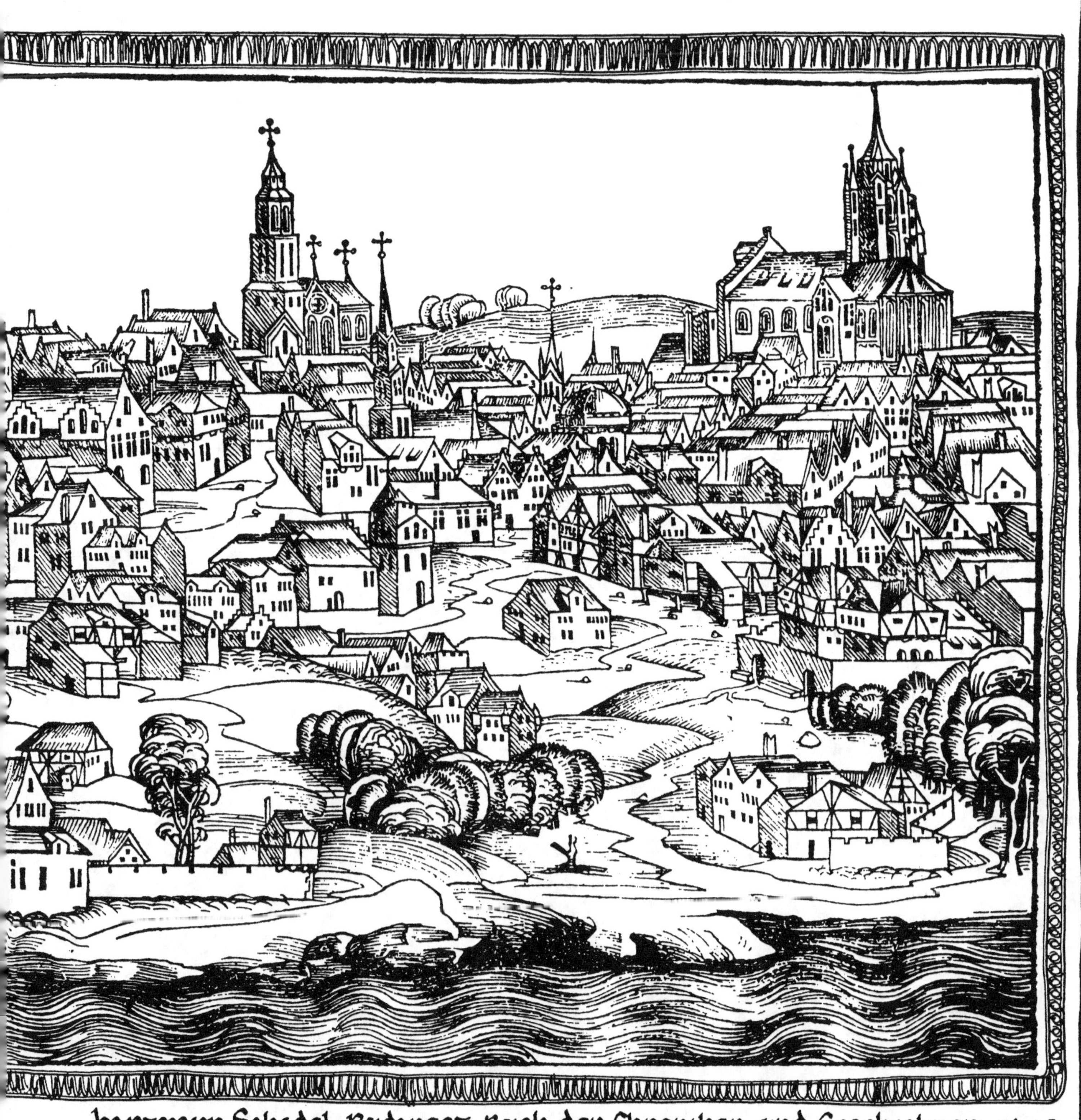

Hartmann Schedel · Budapest · Buch der Chroniken und Geschichten · 1493 ·

www.ingramcontent.com/pod-product-compliance
Lightning Source LLC
LaVergne TN
LVHW080020110826
845148LV00019B/1084

9780865343429